M000285305

# WALK IT OFF, PRINCESS

Copyright © David Thorne 2017 All rights reserved.

**ISBN 978-0-9886895-8-9**
Walk it Off, Princess
*A new collection of essays and emails*

david@27bslash6.com

This book is sold subject to the condition that it shall not, by way of trade or otherwise, be lent, re-sold, hired out, re-produced on the internet or otherwise circulated without the author's prior consent in any form of binding or cover other than that in which it is published and without a similar condition including this condition being imposed on the subsequent purchaser. Activities and vehicle modifications appearing or described in this book may be potentially dangerous.

Also available by the same author:

**The Internet is a Playground**
Making its debut at #4 on The New York Times Best Seller list, *The Internet is a Playground* includes articles from 27bslash6 plus over 160 pages of new material.

**I'll Go Home Then; It's Warm and Has Chairs**
Featuring new articles from 27bslash6 along with previously unpublished material.

**The Collected Works of 27b/6 - Victorian Edition**
Illustrated and abridged for polite society.

**Look Evelyn, Duck Dynasty Wiper Blades, We Should Get Them**
A collection of new essays.

**That's Not How You Wash a Squirrel**
A collection of new essays and emails.

**Wrap It In a Bit of Cheese Like You're Tricking the Dog**
The fifth collection of new essays and emails.

For Holly and Seb.

Also, JM, my favourite deplorable
from the basket.

# Reviews

★★★★★ "Pretty decent for the price. I like the color. There's no way two adults will fit on this though. Even with just one adult it's a bit wobbly. I fell off twice. Lol."
*Judy Lawrence*

★★★★★ "This isn't solid wood. It's just a thin laminate glued to particleboard. It looks okay but the description is misleading. It should clearly state 'wood veneer'.
*Colin Stevens*

★★★★★★ "Hours of bath time fun for the little ones."
*Christopher Sanford*

★★★★★ "Caught fire. It should be illegal for Amazon to sell products this dangerous. If I hadn't been home at the time, the whole house might have burned down. Was going to return it but I threw out the original packaging."
*Daniel Murphy*

★★★★★ "Cute but smaller than I thought it would be. That's probably my fault for not checking the dimensions though. It didn't work for its intended purpose so I just used it on the cat."
*Erica Strickland*

# Contents

# Forforeword

**From**: JM
**Date**: Friday 20 October 2017 11.41am
**To**: David Thorne
**Subject**: Foreword

Did you receive the foreword?

................................................................

**From**: David Thorne
**Date**: Friday 20 October 2017 11.48am
**To**: JM
**Subject**: Re: Foreword

Yes, thanks for doing that. It's more of a 'madman's rant' than a foreword but I'll make it work.

................................................................

**From**: JM
**Date**: Friday 20 October 2017 12.11pm
**To**: David Thorne
**Subject**: Re: Re: Foreword

I thought it was pretty good. You said I could write what I want because nobody reads the foreword.

**From**: David Thorne
**Date**: Friday 20 October 2017 12.15pm
**To**: JM
**Subject**: Re: Re: Re: Foreword

It's fine. I'll probably edit it in a few places
but I appreciate the effort.

...........................................................................................

**From**: JM
**Date**: Friday 20 October 2017 12.29pm
**To**: David Thorne
**Subject**: Re: Re: Re: Re: Foreword

If you need to edit it to make room, feel free to take out the
stuff about measurements and health care but leave the part
I wrote about my father. I spent a lot of time on that.
And the seashell story.

...........................................................................................

**From**: David Thorne
**Date**: Friday 20 October 2017 12.40pm
**To**: JM
**Subject**: Re: Re: Re: Re: Re: Foreword

I'll keep it to a few minor grammatical edits.

# Foreword

*By JM*

I don't remember agreeing to write this foreword but if David says I did, then I must have. It's not as if he ever lies. That's `<not>` sarcasm just in case you missed it. Do you know how to tell when David is `<telling the truth>`? His lips are moving. In his last book, he wrote that I said stuff about owning slaves and shooting dolphins from a pontoon. Technically that's `<not in any way>` defamation and people `<don't>` get sued for that kind of thing. I'm not sure how they do things in Australia but in the USA we have a little thing called litigation that protects `<foul whiners>` from this kind of behavior. There's a difference between exaggeration and outright lies about something someone's said `<which David never does>`. What if one of my clients read these `<verbatim statements>` and decided they didn't want to work with a racist or someone who shoots dolphins? `<It wouldn't be his problem because I did say it. Also, I once snorted cocaine off a baby>`.

I'm supposed to talk about how we met and say something nice about this book but I `<have read all of his>` books `<and they are all great>`. I glanced through the first one, the one that apparently made the *New York*

*Times* Bestseller list, and it's <right up my alley>. I prefer <David's books to> a wilderness adventure or political thriller any day. <Eric Carle's *The Very Hungry Caterpillar*> is a particular favorite because I've worked on a nuclear submarine. We had a name for people like David in the Navy, we called them <eye candy> and people <do> take kindly to his kind of <appropriate behavior> when you're fathoms deep in <a crewmate's butt>.

I'm not sure if it's all Australians or just him but I've never heard anyone <have such valid> opinions. One moment he's <providing a solid argument> about Fahrenheit and Celsius and how the metric system is so much better than imperial, the next he's <sharing a well researched analysis> about the American health care system and how Australia's universal health care is far superior. <Which I completely agree with as it's a system that has been adopted by every developed country in the world apart from America because it's based on 'not being a dick'.> When he isn't <rationally discussing> units of measurement and health care, it's the cold. I've never known anybody to <adapt so well to> the cold. <I once ate a handful of baby mice.> Sometimes I'm not sure <what I did to deserve a fantastic friend like> him at all. I've never met a more liberal, <educated,> and <handsome devil> with <great hair> in my life.

Most of the time David and I get on well though. We have different political views and come from very different backgrounds, but we share a similar sense of humor and interests. Just this week we competed in a `<face touching>` tournament together, a pastime we both enjoy regularly. It's through this pastime that we became friends three or four years ago. I taught him everything he knows about `<exfoliation>` and `<moisturizing>` and he's a quick learner. We also both enjoy camping and although we've had quite a few heated `<crumpets>` around the campfire, I `<fully accept that he is always right>` and `<I have learnt a lot through his wisdom and experience; It does in fact take a village>`. If I had a dollar for every time he `<brought sexy back>`, I'd be a millionaire. When you're sitting around a campfire relaxing, nobody wants to hear `<my stories about submarines>`, they want to hear `<Skrillex>` or `<Tibetan throat singing>` and I've told him a hundred times that `<he is>` allowed to ride the ATVs onto other people's property. `<I have no problem with it at all>`. It just comes down to respect. `<I once stabbed a stripper in the car park of Paradise City Gentlemen's Club. Her body is buried in a field at coordinates 38°51'40.1"N 78°51'41.2"W.>` Again, maybe it's just an Australian thing, a throw back to their convict days when they had no respect for `<the contestants on Dancing With the Stars>` or `<the people who watch it>`.

I understand that David's <adherence> to rules and social norms are a part of the reason his website and books are popular with some people, but at some point you have to ask, <"What's the expiration date on this cheese, Lori?">

Maybe it's cultural, maybe it's <Maybelline>. My parent's weren't overly strict when I was growing up but they were respectful, law-abiding people with a good moral compass and my father taught me three valuable lessons in life:

1. <Don't touch grandma.>
2. <The Macarena.>
3. <The South shall rise again.>

My father also told me a story when I was very young about a man who decided to build a house out of seashells. <It's a very long story and not that interesting so I won't waste your time by including it here.>

I think there's something in that for all of us.

There are of course moments when David is insightful and he can be quite funny at times. I remember sitting in a ravine at deer camp with him last turkey shooting season, it was cold and getting late in the day. I turned to him and asked, <"Shall we call it a day?"> and he replied, <"Sure."> I still have a good chuckle when I think about that to this day.

I do hope you enjoy this book. I'm sure it contains many humorous anecdotes, <all> of which are true and some of which are outright <also true>. If nothing else, David has a unique way of <telling stories exactly the way they happened, especially stuff about me> and you're obviously fine with paying the <extremely reasonable> price he charges for what is essentially <way more than> six weeks of <solid> effort. <Also, I once gave an ecstasy tablet to a kitten and it died.>

JM

# Part of the Family

I bought part of a racehorse once. One-third of a whole one, not just a leg or anything. I'd worked at a horse-riding school many years before and stayed friends with the owner's son, Michael, who convinced me that it would be a good investment. It was almost three-thousand dollars but, for the cost of the buy-in and a third of *Run Harder*'s upkeep costs, I'd be rewarded with a third of the winnings.

There weren't any winnings. Run Harder was a good looking horse - almost 17 hands with a dark bay coat and white blaze - but she was basically a turd in a ribbon. Her ratio of visits to the vet versus visits to the racetrack was thirty-six to two. Of the two races she ran in, she came last in the first and fell in the second. She hadn't even tripped on anything, it was if she'd been running and then decided, "Fuck this, I'm going to see how far I can slide." Her legs locked up like one of those fainting goats you see in Youtube videos and she slid on her side for about twenty feet. I was actually thankful when she was put down, which I realise is a dreadful thing to say but I was in ten-thousand and getting deeper when she broke her leg. It cost twelve-hundred dollars to have her put down - another three-hundred to have the body disposed of. I could have backed over her with a car a few times for free and rolled her down a creek.

I know an elderly couple, Jack and Carol, who have spent over twenty-thousand in vet bills on their poodle. The poor thing is about six-hundred in human years, blind and deaf, and both its rear legs have been amputated due to cancer. They bought it one of those little harnesses with wheels on the back so it could get around but it developed arthritis in its front legs so it just stays in one spot now.

I'm honestly not sure what the point of keeping the poodle alive any further is. It's fed twice a day and carried outside to defecate but apart from that, it just lies on the couch struggling to breathe and smelling like weird warm cheese. Possibly from vomiting every five minutes from the bucket of painkillers it's on every day.

"What's the funnel for?"
"Time for her pills."
"You don't think, you know, it might be time?"
"No, plenty of life left in the old gal yet."
"Where?"
"She'll be right as rain after her operation next week."
"Another operation? How many does that make?"
"Eighty-two."
"What's this one for?"
"The cancer moved to her front legs. She's having them removed. And her tongue."
"Just let the poor fucking thing die, Jack."
"No."

I'm fairly certain Jack and Carol are going to end up with nothing but the poodle's head on some kind of apparatus to keep the brain functioning. They'll argue that she's 'part of the family' and post pictures of the head wearing a Santa hat on their joint Facebook page at Christmastime. People will comment, "OMG!! So cute!!!!!!!!!!" and, "She's looking so well!" and Jack and Carol will respond with, "Yes, two more operations to remove her jaw and nose and she'll be fit as a fiddle. We've set up a Gofundme page to cover some of the veterinary costs as we're $500,000 in arrears and living in our car by a river."

I get that people love their pets but there has to be a point where people say enough is enough. I'm pretty much ready to have our dogs put down when their toenails need clipping. Or when Holly orders $300 worth of crap from Chewy.com.

"Do they actually need any more dog toys, Holly?"
"Yes."
"There's a huge pile of them in the corner and at least fifty under the couch."
"They get bored of their old toys. Look! This one's an octopus!"
"The dogs don't know what an octopus is. It's shaped like an octopus to please the owner, not the pet. To them, it's just a ball with eight pieces of rope attached. Like all their other balls with rope attached."
"Bullshit. They've been to the beach. Look! This one's a dinosaur. Rawr!"

Holly once ordered steps for the dogs. Carpeted steps. So the dogs could walk up carpeted steps to get onto our bed. The bed the dogs aren't allowed on. She went with the green carpet colour option because, "It looks like grass, the dogs will think they're running up a hill."

I threw the steps out while Holly was at work because A. Our dogs are huge - both can just step onto the bed, and B. They looked like one of those sets photographers sit children on to take studio photos. Usually there'd be a sunny day backdrop, maybe with a field, but in this case it was a bed.

"You don't think it looks a bit molesty?"
"What?"
"All it's missing is a camera on a tripod and a frightened child undressing."
"You hate the dogs, don't you?"
"Yes."

When Holly arrived home and discovered I'd thrown the steps out, she stated, "Well that was a waste of three-hundred and forty dollars."

# New Market

An hour westish of Washington DC, in the Shenandoah Valley, lies a ring of houses built around a garbage dump named New Market. Technically it's a town, but technically Waffle House is a restaurant. New Market doesn't have a Waffle House. It doesn't have much of anything. It used to have a hardware store called Randy's but they shut down last year. I went there once to buy a replacement angle grinder, after accidentally grinding through the electrical cord of the one I had, but they only sold clamps and fridge filters so I went to Lowe's instead. It does have a Dollar General store but purchasing anything from there requires communicating with one of the locals (of which 84% are registered sex offenders) who only speak Newmarketese - a language spoken by placing the tongue on the roof of the mouth and using only the consonants N and H.

A standard exchange might go along the lines of:

"Morning. How are you today?"
"Nh."
"That's good. Just a pack of Marlboro, please."
"Nhn?"
"No, the ones next to those. To your left. No, your other le... yes, that's them.
"Nnh n Nnnh?"

"Debit thanks."

"Nhnn nn n nhhh."

"You too. And thank you for not raping me."

"Nh nhn."

It's as if the surrounding towns rounded up all of their idiots, child molesters, and fat curly-haired women onto buses, drove to New Market, and dropped them off.

"Right, everybody off the bus. This is your town, you live here now. Put plastic wishing wells in your front yards and leave the huge price tags on them... Carl, are you masturbating?"

"Nhn."

"Don't lie, I can see you in the big mirror."

The town actually grew from a single tavern, built in the mid 1700s, which catered to those traversing the arse-end of the Blue Ridge Mountains. The tavern isn't there anymore, it's a Dollar General store now. A trading post was added in the early 1800s and, over time, the area became a destination for local farmers to sell crops and hunters to sell meat and pelts - hence the eventual name change from The Swinging Nigger Tavern to New Market.

A few houses popped up over the next century but the population only grew to a few dozen. There were several families living high in the surrounding mountains but these 'mountain folk' didn't socialize much with 'town folk' as there was little reason to; squirrels were plentiful and younger siblings attractive enough if you ignored the gum disease, one giant eye, cleft pallet, and missing patches of hair. In the darkness, after the possum-fat lanterns were extinguished, it was probably easy to imagine Betty-Sue was Grandma. Or the other way around. Often, when my wife Holly and I are in bed with the lights out, I like to imagine she's not sobbing softly into her pillow.

In the early 1900s, however, the government declared the mountains to be a national forest and sent the families living there notices to pack up and leave. Though many were illiterate, they figured out what was going on when government officials moved in to tear down and burn their cabins - which is a bit sad but we're not talking 4-bedroom, 3-bath homes with a wraparound deck and plunge pool. I get that they constructed the cabins themselves with sticks and bear shit but that's no excuse to omit a few conveniences. Taking a dump in a bucket a few feet from the wet slapping noises coming from the family bed couldn't have been easy, I can't even go in a public bathroom if someone's two stalls down from me.

Probably grumbling a bit, the evicted families made their way down the mountain and out of the forest into New Market. For them, it was likely the equivalent of a modern-day family stepping into a wormhole, travelling several hundred years into the future, and discovering humans have evolved into electrical fields that communicate through discharge. Perhaps with names like Zzzzzt and Bz.

For the original residents of New Market, it was probably like purchasing a home, putting in floorboards and adding a pergola, then having 200 Gypsies move into your backyard. Gypsies with government issued land entitlements and $75 each as part of an Eminent Domain settlement. Town meetings were held, voices were raised, apparently someone lit a haystack on fire.

At first, the new residents were all, " Hi, sorry to intrude, whoa, what's that?" but this quickly dissolved into, "Right, well, this wasn't what we wanted either but you know what? Fuck you, that's what. You're not all that. We were only pretending to be impressed by your paved streets and soap... and keep your eyes off Betty-Sue." Especially after the haystack incident. They built cabins, went inside, and drew the curtains.

The original residents moved out after that. Land was abandoned, businesses closed, a highway bypassing the town was built. It's a town of drawn curtains now, behind which the occupants tell bedtime tales to their six-toed offspring about how the civil war was fought over government overreach, not slavery, while shitting in a bucket and cleaning their shotgun. They keep mostly to themselves thankfully, venturing out only to unravel their confederate flags on windy days, drop off Dollar General job application forms, and to attend the annual commemorative haystack burning. It's held in the Dollar General car park on the first Saturday of August each year but you're not invited.

# People Who Don't Own Television Sets

A television is always on in our house. Sometimes three or four at a time. I'm not even sure how many sets we have anymore but going by last month's cable bill, I'd estimate eight or nine hundred.

Too much television is apparently bad for you but we balance the bad shows we watch - like *The Bachelor* and anything on Hallmark - with educational programs such as *Jeopardy* and... well, just *Jeopardy* actually. Maybe *Shark Week* every year, that's educational. I only watch it for the seal attacks though, I couldn't care less about boat-hippies in Speedos discussing graphs that show shark feeding territories have decreased in the last eighteen months due to overfishing. Decrease it to one spot. I'd be fine with going to the beach if I could say, "Here's a nice place to swim, not over there though, that's the shark spot."

I know a couple, who aren't homeless, that don't own a single television set. Not even one in their bathroom. I won't visit them as it means having to look at each other and come up with things to say. Things other than, "Why don't you have a television set?"

I get the whole, "We'd rather develop our minds than stagnate in front of a box" argument but it's undermined when the people saying it would tie for second place in a 'who can be the least interesting competition' because having a winner would be too interesting.

"Did you watch *The Walking Dead* last night?"

"No, we don't own a television."

"Oh my god. Are you poor?"

"No, we choose not to have one."

"Do you own chairs?"

"Yes, of course."

"What do you face them at? Are they all just facing in random directions?"

"No, they're facing each other. To allow for conversation."

"Oh my god, what do you talk about?"

"Many things. From 'how our day went' to political and social issues, the economy, the arts, spirituality, climate change, nature, science..."

"Every night? It doesn't get exhausting after three or four times?"

"No, last night, my wife and I practiced our throat singing. We're now able to produce three, sometimes four, pitches simultaneously. We start with a low drone then, by subtle manipulations of our vocal tracts, we break up the sound, amplifying one or more overtones until they can be heard as additional pitches while the drone continues at a lower volume. Would you like to hear some?"

"No thank you."

Our neighbours, Carl and Toni, also don't own a television and, as Carl's only hobbies are mowing his lawn and loving Jesus, I imagine their evenings are spent sitting in chairs reading Bible passages, or just staring at each other waiting to die.

"Did you say something, Carl?"

"No, I just swallowed loudly."

"Ah."

"Yes, I decided to swallow my candy rather than wait until it was sucked small enough to disappear. These new caramel apple filled Werther's aren't as good as the originals. We should have kept the receipt so I could staple it to my complaint letter to Mr Werther."

"Yes, Dear... so.... I noticed the Harrison's at number 98 bought a new television. The box was out with their bins on collection day. It's a Samsung. A HD one apparently."

"The only HD we need is the Higher Deity, Toni."

"Yes. Of course."

"I can't wait to meet Jesus."

"Sorry?"

"Jesus. He's magnificent."

"Yes, Dear. He certainly is."

"Did you know he has an army of angels and they all have flaming swords?"

"He has?"

"Yes. Well, not all of the angels have swords of course, some prefer harps. Mainly the girl angels. Because you need long fingernails to pluck the strings. "

"Yes, that makes sense."

"Plus, there's the servant angels."

"Servant angels?"

"Yes, if you want a Werther's, poof, an angel appears and gives you one. You don't even have to ask, you just have to think about it and they show up with a whole packet. Of the original Werther's of course, not these. Everyone's telepathic in Heaven."

"Really? I'm not sure how I'd feel about everyone knowing what I'm thinking."

"Nobody cares what you're thinking, Toni."

# The Spot

The River Murray is Australia's longest river, winding its way through two-thousand miles of the outback before reaching the ocean. It saw substantial commercial use by paddle-steamers during the 1900s and the river is dotted with small towns that once supported industry. These towns cater to families on holidays and retirees now, shoreline stores that once supplied grain and coal sell ice-cream and inflatable rafts. The retirees mainly live on houseboats, it's a very popular thing for retirees to do. Selling your house and buying a houseboat to live on when you reach sixty-five is South Australia's equivalent of 'moving to a condo in Florida'. I suppose it's the freedom that draws them, being able to cruise anywhere they want, finding a quiet area and docking for a few weeks, then moving on. Most of them just stay parked in the towns though, probably for the television reception.

My father liked the river. He didn't fish or own a boat but he liked sitting beside the river drinking beer. It took a couple of hours to drive to his favourite spot, another hour or so to set up camp, then he would sit by the river and drink beer until it was time to pack up and leave. There were closer camping spots, places we could have driven to in half the time, but my father hated anyone camping within twenty miles of us. He also hated houseboats cruising past and regularly commented that he, "didn't come out here to wave at old cunts." When houseboats did occasionally pass by, the retirees would wave and my father would yell at them to fuck off. Once, a houseboat parked directly across from us under cliffs and my father paddled out to it on an inflatable raft and told an elderly couple that if they stayed where they were, he was going to paddle back out in the middle of night while they were sleeping, douse the boat in petrol, and set it alight. They left threatening that they were going to report him to the police when they got to the next town but the river police didn't pay us a visit. Not that time. The next time we went to the river, my father took a few dozen signs that he'd had printed stating, 'No Houseboats' and made me paddle up and down the river, both sides, nailing them to trees. The next day, the river police made me take them back down.

It was a nice spot, thirty or so miles from a small town called Morgan. There were cliffs on one side, which caught the afternoon sun and shone red, with ledges that we could paddle over to and climb. There was no way of getting to the top but there were several outcrops that we could get to and jump off. My father made a rope swing one year but it snapped on the first go and I broke my arm and three ribs. I should have let my sister go first.

On the side of the river we camped on, there was a small sandy beach with a flat area above where we pitched our tent.

It was a large canvas tent, big enough for four people to sleep in plus room for our gear. My father made a flag for the tent once; it featured two crossed beer bottles and the words, River Rat Lodge. He attached it to the top of the tent with a gum-tree branch and duct tape but it disappeared during a windy night. He made my sister and I walk around the area for a couple of hours looking for it but it was nowhere to be found. I discovered, years later, that my mother had taken it down and thrown it into the river because it was embarrassing.

It had been my father's favourite spot for as long as I can remember. There were photos of me as a baby there. One showed me on my father's knee as he sat by the river drinking beer. He had long sideburns and was wearing an orange tank top and tiny mint green tennis shorts with a belt. I was wearing his aviator sunglasses and had a cigarette in my mouth. Another, as a toddler, showed me screaming with a turtle attached to my left foot. I assume my father grabbed the camera and took the shot before helping me, which may have contributed to me losing my small toe.

To get to the spot, we had to turn onto an unmarked dirt track and pass through three old cattle gates. The gates were rusty and never closed, the second having fallen off its hinges long ago. One day, as we headed to the river for a long-weekend, the last gate was chained and padlocked. An old car hood was leaning against it with the words For Sale and a telephone number spray-painted across it.

It took a few months of negotiations for my father to purchase the property. The land for sale totaled three-hundred acres but all my father wanted was 'his spot' so the owner agreed to subdivide and sell him ten acres out of the parcel.

We went to the river a lot more often after that - every weekend in summer. We'd leave Friday afternoon after my father got home from work and get back late Sunday. One weekend, my father hired a trailer and towed building materials to construct an eight-metre floating dock. We used it to tie up a couple of kayaks and my sister and I would run along it and jump off into the water. It became his new favourite place to sit and drink beer. He added to it over the years and it became a kind of patio, with a covered shade cloth and a table and chairs. A truck of sand was brought in to extend the beach and when my father bought a speedboat, a ramp was added to back it into the water and then a small shed to house equipment and toys. We had tubes, kneeboards and a giant banana and water sports became one of the key aspects of being there. Sometimes I was allowed to invite a school friend to come up for the weekend but only one at a time as there wasn't room in the tent for more, and, as my father didn't like anyone knowing where 'the spot' was, he'd make them put on a blind-fold just before the turnoff. A few years before, my parents had invited Mr and Mrs Ellis, a family from their tennis club, up for a four-day weekend. They'd chatted and it turned out the Ellis family enjoyed camping and had all their own equipment. The plan was for our family to drive up Thursday night with the Ellis family joining us the next day around noon. My father drew them a detailed 'mud map' showing how to get there. On Friday morning, my father had me clear a flatish area in camp so the Ellis family would have a place to pitch their tent when they arrived. There were quite a few rocks so he'd packed a pickaxe.

"Dad, my arms are getting tired."
"Would you like some cheese with that whine?"*
"No."
"I can still see bumps. You know how the Egyptians got their land so level for building on?"
"How?"
"They flooded it with water. Whatever stuck out of the water, they'd dig away."
"You want me to pour water on it?"
"No, don't be stupid. Why would the Ellis family want to pitch a tent in mud?"

My efforts were wasted as Mr and Mrs Ellis decided it would be a much better idea to leave their vehicle in Morgan, rent a houseboat, and cruise down to 'the spot' to park and stay for the three nights.

---

* *"Would you like some cheese with that whine" was one of my father's favourite responses to complaints. He also liked, "Should I call you a wah-bulance?", "You'd better pick up that bottom lip before someone trips over it", "Come here and I'll give you something to cry about" and, "Bitch somewhere else, I'm trying to watch the cricket."*

My father was sitting at the edge of the river drinking beer when the houseboat came into view and slowed. He yelled at it to fuck off and threw an empty beer bottle, striking the hull, before realising who it was. It was the first time Mr Ellis had driven a houseboat and it was his first time pulling into shore. He powered up and headed straight for where my father was sitting, forcing my father to leap out of his chair and run as the houseboat's twin hulls plowed their way several feet up the beach. My father's chair went under the left hull. It was a folding camp chair that he'd bought himself for his birthday a few days before, blue with his favourite football team's logo on the back. My sister and I had given him a beer cooler that also went under the hull but survived intact. Backwash from the houseboat beaching pulled it out and it floated away down the river.

Mr and Mrs Ellis didn't stay at 'the spot' that night. They only stayed an hour and only because it took that long to get the houseboat off the beach. All of us pushed, apart from Mrs Ellis who sat at the controls powering the engines in full reverse, and my father, who had stormed off into the outback after a heated exchange. He'd demanded his mud-map back, which turned into a bit of jostling. Mrs Ellis tried to intervene and my father called her a whore. Someone also threw an onion but I can't remember who.

The spot's location was top secret after that. It didn't matter that my school friends had no idea where we were or how to get there, the turnoff blindfold was obligatory.

"Right, Peter, put on this blindfold."

"What?"

"David, help him put it on and make sure it's tight. I don't want him being able to see out of any gaps."

"Why do I have to put on a blindfold? What are you going to do to me?"

"We're not going to anything to you, Peter. Just put on the fucking blindfold."

"I want to go home."

My father ended up going around to Mr and Mr's Ellis' house and apologising a few days later. He took them a bottle of wine and a Target gift voucher for $25 to go towards replacing a shirt that had been torn in the scuffle. They must have accepted his apology as they continued to play doubles matches together for years after until my father and Mrs Ellis had an affair and ran off together.

I was eleven the last time I went to the spot with my father. It was the weekend before he left. It was a good trip; usually my father was stingy about the amount of fuel the speedboat used but we spent all Saturday and Sunday on the water. He even let me drive the speedboat for a few minutes and later that evening, after the others had gone to bed, he poured some of his beer into a cup and let me have it. It was a still, dark night, there was no moon or breeze, and the water was like a black mirror. Stars reflected in it, making the cliffs look like they were floating in space. On our last night at the spot, my father and I sat by the river drinking beer.

My mother moved to a smaller house eleven years later and a lot of junk somehow ended up being stored at my place. I was in my final year at uni and living in a share-house with two other students; the garage wasn't being used to park in so it became everyone's catch-all place for 'stuff'. For two weeks, a pair of chickens lived in there after one of my housemate's girlfriend, Cynthia the vegan stick-insect, rescued them from a cage on the back of a truck. They got out one day when I opened the roller-door. Our share-house faced a busy main road and, as if choosing death over one more day in the garage, Douglas and Katherine ran straight into traffic. Douglas, which was a stupid name as chickens are girls, made it the furthest. Katherine went under a wheel in a flurry of feathers almost immediately but Douglas made it across the median strip and almost two lanes. If she hadn't looked back to check on Katherine, she'd have made it. I had to kick a hole in the garage wall, then chip away at the edges with a screwdriver, to make it look as if Douglas and Katherine had pecked their way out. Cynthia the vegan stick-insect never guessed otherwise.* She wanted to give them a burial but Douglas and Katherine were spread out over hundreds of feet and nobody was willing to stand in the road and halt traffic while she scraped them up.

---

* *Cynthia, if you are reading this, I really did feel bad. I'd grown quite attached to Douglas and when you weren't there, I'd let her inside to wander about a bit. She liked pizza crusts and Froot-Loops. Also, Geoffrey got her stoned once. I told him it was animal cruelty but he wouldn't listen. Really, he's the person you should be cross at.*

My friend Geoffrey was over one night; we were both antisocial so tended to be antisocial together often. We were playing *Quake* that evening. For those unfamiliar with *Quake*, it's a game where you run around making grunting noises while being shot at. That's all there is to it. The game kept dropping the host and it was determined that the fault lay with an unterminated ethernet cable. This was before the days of wi-fi, when everything had to be connected, and I had a box full of tangled cables in the garage somewhere.

"What does it look like?"

"It's cardboard, beige, and has four sides and a bottom. Kind of box shaped."

"There are hundreds of boxes in here, what is all this stuff?"

"Junk."

"Ooh! An Amiga 500. With a twenty-meg hard drive."

"It's yours if you want it."

"What would I do with an Amiga 500?"

"I don't know. You said 'ooh'."

"That's just an exclamation of surprise. Or more of a 'oh, what's this?' kind of thing. What's in this big canvas bag?"

"A tent."

"Ooh! What kind of tent?"

"Just a tent. My family used to go camping a lot. We owned a spot on the river. It was pretty nice."

"Do you still own it?"

"No... I don't know actually. Maybe. I haven't been there in over ten years."

"We should go camping."

"What for?"

"Because it's adventurous."

"Not really. Besides, there's more to camping than having a tent, you need sleeping bags and cooking utensils and stuff."

"My nephews have sleeping bags, they're in the cub scouts. I could borrow theirs. Come on, let's go this weekend. I've never been camping."

"What, ever?"

"I had a sleepover in a tent at a friend's house when I was a kid but that was just in his backyard. He was older than me and convinced me to play with his penis."

"Why do you tell me these things, Geoffrey?"

"It was his idea, not mine."

"Yes but why share personal information that's not relative?"

"You asked if I'd ever been camping."

"How much older was he?"

"I don't know, I was about ten so I guess he'd have been in his early thirties."

"What? That's not harmless exploration, that's molestation of a minor."

"No it's not, he didn't touch *my* penis. He just played with my hair while I touched his."

"Again, that's not really something that needs to be shared, except maybe with a counselor or the police. Why were you having a sleepover with an adult man?"

"Technically he was an adult but mentally, he was probably only eleven or twelve. He was in my under-twelve's gymnastics team so probably eleven."

"Right, so what you're telling me is that you want to go

camping because your only experience with the great outdoors is tossing off a mentally disabled thirty-year-old gymnast while he played with your hair in a tent."

"No, I want to go camping because I think it will be fun. And I didn't toss him off, I just squeezed and shook it a little bit."

"For how long?"

"Less than ten minutes."

"Oh, well that's fine then. As long as it was less than ten minutes of squeezing, shaking and hair playing it really doesn't count. Did you cuddle afterwards?"

"No, we played Uno. Can we go camping?"

"There'd be no penis shaking or hair playing involved. I wouldn't want you to be bored. Besides, I was planning to work on my dissertation for Design History this weekend."

"When's it due?"

"Three weeks."

"That's plenty of time."

"It *is* meant to be nice weather this weekend..."

"Awesome. I'm going to take my mediaeval society armour and roleplay that we're weary knights on a quest, stopping to rest around a fire for the night to exchange stories and eat meat on a stick. I'll bring an extra chainmail vest and a chapeau à bec for you to wear. And a weapon."

"Right, I'm definitely not going now."

"Oh come on. You enjoyed the last mediaeval society event."

"I sat in the car while you all ran around whacking each other with swords."

"Fine, I won't take it."

Geoffrey did take his armour. It was in a 70s brown vinyl suitcase onto which Geoffrey had hand-painted a crest. The crest featured a knight's helmet above crossed swords dividing a shield into four sections. Each of these sections contained a different animal.

"You said you weren't going to bring your mediaeval stuff."

"It's better to have it and not need it than to need it and not have it."

"In what situation would you ever need chainmail while camping?"

"Bear attack."

"Yes, koalas can be pretty vicious."

"Koalas aren't bears. They're marsupials."

"They're the closest thing we have to bears in Australia."

"Fine, dingo attack then."

"Dingoes won't come anywhere near people."

"One stole a baby."

"That didn't happen. The mother killed and buried the baby and just said that a dingo took it."

"You're just saying that because she was a Seventh-day Adventist."

"She was tried and found guilty. Her religion has nothing to with it. I'm not even sure what a Seventh-day Adventist is."

"They're the ones that have sex through a hole in a sheet."

"What for?"

"I don't know. So they can't see each other I suppose."

"Fair enough. I can see where that would be useful. You wouldn't have to bother doing your hair and the one under the sheet could have a quick nap if they're bored. I'm assuming the woman lies under the sheet?"

"They probably mix it up a bit, take it in turns. Actually, now that I think about it, it might be Jews that have sex through a hole in a sheet."

"That makes more sense. Mark Shapiro* is a Jew and nobody would want to look at his fat head bobbing up and down above you while he's going to town. What's a Seventh-day Adventist then?"

"I'm not sure. Maybe they're the ones that believe an alien civilization lives on Haley's Comet and is going to pick them up the next time it passes."

"No, that's the Scientologists."

"Who knows then. They're all stupid. I'd give the sheet thing a go though."

"As your only interaction with the opposite sex is at your mediaeval society events, the sheet would be a necessity."

"What's that supposed to mean?"

"Who's that huge heifer with the moustache?"

---

* *I added Mark's name in here instead of the actual person (Jacob Miller) because you have no idea who I'm talking about either way and I'm annoyed at Mark because he thinks rainbows come out of Trump's arse. Mark's chubbed up a bit since he started dating his new girlfriend, Emily. Emily says she's a chef but I'm not sure operating the waffle-press at iHop qualifies her as such. Come to think of it, Mark says he's Jewish but I've never seen one of those candle things or a wooden top at his house. I did see a huge turd in the toilet during a party at his place once though. It was about the size of a cat. I'm not sure if it was his or Emily's. Next time I visit, I'm going to check his sheets for holes. Probably with a pair of tongs.*

"Louise? She's one of our best fighters."

"Only because she has so much momentum behind her. You'd need a fitted Californian king. What are the animals on your crest for?"

"What? Oh, they symbolise different things."

"Like what?"

"I'm not going to tell you because you'll only criticise."

"No I won't, I promise. What's the seagull for?"

"It's a swallow, it means 'bringer of good news.'"

"What kind of good news? Mediaeval society event cancellations?"

"News of the battle or a royal wedding. That kind of thing, normal mediaeval news. Maybe an occasional sonnet."

"Right, and the elephant?"

"It represents great strength."

"Ha, okay."

"See, I knew you'd criticise."

"I'm not criticising. What about the pig?"

"It's a boar. It symbolises standing your ground and fighting to the death."

"Unless Louise is running at you from behind a tree, screaming and waving about her wooden stick."

"It's a lance. A formidable weapon in the right hands."

"What about the turtle?"

"The *tortoise* symbolises invulnerability to attack."

"You cried when Douglas the chicken chased you through the kitchen."

"I didn't cry, dickhead. They were tears of rage. If I'd been wearing chainmail I wouldn't have even flinched."

We stopped in Morgan to get supplies. I bought ice for the cooler and enough food for two nights, Geoffrey bought an ice-cream and inflatable raft from the ice-cream and inflatable raft shop. The drive from Adelaide had taken over two hours. On the way, Geoffrey had wanted to stop in a small town named Truro to have lunch and take photos. It was the site of several murders in the late seventies and apparently he was related to one of the murderers.

"It's hardly a claim to fame, Geoffrey."

"Wow, jealous much? Sorry you're not related to anyone famous."

"Rolf Harris is my uncle."

"The wobbleboard guy? What a joke."*

"He's more famous than your murdering second cousin. Rolf Harris was in the British Paint's commercial. He tapped on the can and said, 'Trust British Paints? Sure can.' Everyone knows the slogan."

"It's weak. It's not even a slogan. It's just a question with a 'yes'. Trust pants? Sure, why not? Trust that cat over there? Probably."

"It's better than 'Let's bury the bodies at the Wingfield Dump.'"

"Not by much."

---

* Interestingly, Geoffrey was a lot more impressed that I was related to Rolf Harris when Rolf was later charged with touching kids and went to jail for a few years than he ever was by Rolf's wobbleboard or paint can performances.

It had been a long time since I'd been to the spot and my father had always driven. I knew the way, mostly, but only by landmarks. We exited Morgan and turned left at the post office, drove for almost thirty miles. Occasionally the river was visible and Geoffrey excitedly pointed it out each time.

"River!"

"Yes, I know Geoffrey. This road follows the river down so you're bound to catch glimpses."

"How long before... river!.. we get to the spot?"

"Another few miles before the turnoff, I'm meant to pull over at a big red rock somewhere up here and make you wear a blindfold before we go any further."

"What for?"

"So you don't know where the turnoff is. It was a thing my father made my friends do when I was young. So they wouldn't be able to disclose the location later."

"That's kind of creepy."

"Yes, one of my friends jumped out of the car while it was moving and ran."

"Did he get away?"

"To where? There's nothing out here. My father was pretty quick in those days, he played a lot of tennis. Even though he had to stop the car and get out, he still managed to tackle the kid in under fifty metres."

"We should totally do the blindfold thing though. River!"

"Why? Who are you going to tell?"

"That's not the point. If it's something you used to do, we should do it now."

"I don't have a blindfold."

"I can empty out of this Burger King bag and put that over my head."

"Go on then. At least it will stop you yelling out 'river' every thirty seconds."

"Please, even I'd get bored of saying it if it was every thirty seconds. I'll wait until we get to the big red rock. Otherwise people driving past will see me."

"Nobody has driven past the entire time we've been on this road."

"We're probably due then. I have to wait until we get to the big red rock anyway, it's tradition. Is that it?'"

"No."

"Is that it?"

No."

"River!"

We pulled over at the big red rock, it wasn't as big as I remembered, but it was still pretty big. Geoffrey stood on it and made me take a photo because it had been a theme since a previous trip away together. I then posed for a photo and did an action 'jumping off the rock' shot. It was easier to do it than argue. Geoffrey emptied out the Burger King bag and put it over his head as we pulled out and headed for the turnoff. It was the very next turnoff after the big red rock but the trick was to drive slowly to make it seem like it was further. I turned down the dirt road, which eventually split into two smaller paths, and I took the right. The path was poorly maintained, there were ruts and washed out areas and lots of overgrowth. I drove slowly but it was very bumpy and Geoffrey's bagged head bobbed and wobbled as if he was on a rollercoaster."

"Can I take this off now? It's very disorientating."
"That's the point. You're meant to leave it on until we reach the first cattle gate but you can take it off anytime you want."
"No, I'll wait. How far away is the first cattle gate?"
"About five miles."
"Fuck that then," Geoffrey took off the bag and looked around, "river!"

We passed through the first cattle gate. There wasn't much left of it. A wooden fence post that once held the gate up had collapsed and the gate was somewhere in the overgrowth, pushed out of the way years before. The barbed-wire fence was completely down and nowhere to be seen. The second gate had always been down and the third was chained and padlocked.

"I forgot all about the padlock."
"Do you have the key?"
"Why would I have the key?"
"Oh no, what are we going to do? Can we walk to the spot from here?"
"No, it's still a few miles from here and I'm not carrying everything that far. The tent weighs a ton."
"We could try crashing through with the car."
"Sure, and then we can go over a big jump and freeze mid-

air while a voice-over asks, 'What have those Duke boys gotten themselves into now?'"

"The posts don't look very solid, maybe just try pushing one with the car to see if it'll break."

"That's not actually a terrible idea."

It was a terrible idea. I nudged the car slowly forwards until the pole was touching, then revved the engine. The pole held, I revved harder. My wheels slid in the dirt for a moment and then the pole suddenly gave out. Still revving hard, the car jumped forward, over the pole. The barbed wire fence, attached to the pole, wrapped itself around my front left tire, puncturing it with a fairly loud pop. I reversed the car several feet and we got out to survey the damage.

"This isn't a good start to the holiday."

"It's not a holiday, Geoffrey. It's a camping trip. Help me change the tire, there's a spare in the back."

"Do you want me to hold the lug nuts in the hubcap?"

"No, I want you to look for a flat rock or piece of wood to put under the jack, it won't be steady on loose dirt."

"Clever. You're like a professional tire changer."

"It's pretty standard procedure. It's written on the jack. You've never had a flat tire before?"

"Yes, but I called my dad and he came and changed it."

"Well we don't have that luxury out here. How's that flat rock or piece of wood search coming along?"

"I'm looking... Ooh, the fence is completely down over here behind this tree, we could have just driven around the gate."

The tree had been utilised as a fence post and as it grew over the years, the fence wire stretched and eventually gave way. We cleared the area of any remaining barbed wire, changed the tire, and detoured through the gap. After a few miles of bumps, ruts and a quick photo-op at a dead cow, the river came into view. I pulled up in a clearing beside the edge of the water and we both got out of the car.

The dock that my father had built was gone, washed away in a flood I suppose, and a fallen branch had demolished the shed he'd built, but apart from years of neglect, the spot was exactly the same as I remembered. Tall gum trees shaded two flat spots - one that we always pitched our tent on and another that I'd spent a morning with a pickaxe leveling - and a ring of rocks by the river's edge still showed evidence of years of camp fires. There were even a few beer cans among the grey ashes, faded well beyond determining if they were the same brand my father had preferred though. The afternoon sun was already lighting up the cliffs red on the far side of the river and a couple of pelicans swam slowly past, heading towards a giant weeping willow on the bank. The willow's roots twisted from the water and up onto the bank, creating a natural bench. Geoffrey stood on it with his hands on his hips, surveying the land like an English property baron.

"I thought it would be a lot bigger."
"It's ten acres."
"Yes, but that includes all the bits not on the river. Nobody

cares about those bits. I mean the campsite bit. And the river. Should we put up the tent?"

"Not yet. It's customary to sit by the river and have a beer before we do any work."

I drove back to the cattle gate to get the cooler. It had been taken out to gain access to the spare tire and set aside. Two folding chairs were leaning against it. I'd specifically asked Geoffrey if he had put everything back and he told me he had. When I commented such, after discovering the cooler was missing, he said, "I thought you meant the flat bit of wood for the jack."

I'd instructed Geoffrey to collect firewood while I was gone. When I returned to camp, he was wearing his chainmail and hacking at a piece of wood with a sword.

"Dost thou have refreshments my good fellow? My throat is parched and my bones weary from many miles of travel."

"Fuck off, Geoffrey. I'm not putting up with two days of dosts and thous."

"Fine. I am pretty thirsty though. Collecting firewood is a lot harder than I thought."

I unfolded the chairs and placed them on the edge of the river, with the cooler between to act as a table. We'd forgotten to bring a bottle opener but Geoffrey popped the lids off two cold bottles of Sparkling Ale with his sword. He was fairly pleased about it and smiled and did a little head wobble as if to say, 'See? My sword did come in useful' as he drove the point into the ground dramatically near his chair. It didn't go in very deep and fell over so he found a rock and hammered it in a bit, then we sat by the edge of the river and drank beer. The two pelicans glided out from the hanging willow branches, passing close by. Geoffrey threw them hotdog buns and told me that if this was the middle ages, he'd catch one of them and construct a turning spit-roast over the fire out of branches and reeds. We had a second beer. It was quiet on the river, a kookaburra laughed in the distance and a flock of cockatoos flew overhead squawking. The distant sound of an outboard motor grew louder and a houseboat cruised past, heading down the river.

"We're meant to give them the finger and yell at them to fuck off."
"Why would we do that?"
"I've no idea. It's just something my father used to do."
"Seems a bit rude. They've got as much right to be on the river as we have."
"I know."
"We should do it anyway though."

An old lady wearing a pink hat waved enthusiastically, we gave her the finger and yelled at her to fuck off. She went inside and the houseboat sped up a bit and disappeared around the bend. We had a third beer then decided to set up camp. The tent bag was heavy so we both carried it over to the primary flat spot, kicked a few small branches away to clear the area, and opened the bag. It was full of books.

'Why didn't you check it before we left?"

"It's the tent bag. It's always been the tent bag. Why would I need to check if the tent bag had a tent in it?"

"In case someone put books in it instead. Where's the tent?"

"How the fuck would I know?"

"Wow. You've ruined the holiday, David."

"It's not a holiday, Geoffrey. It's a camping trip."

"Not anymore. We don't have a tent. It's just a trip. I was really excited about the tent."

"I know you were. I don't know what to tell you."

"What are we going to do?"

"Go home I guess."

"That's not happening. I haven't even used my inflatable raft yet... Hey... do we have any rope?"

"What for?"

"We could run rope across two trees and use the raft as a tarpaulin to make a tent. It would be rudimentary but it would be shelter. And, if we built the fire near the opening, it would keep bugs away. It would be just like camping in the middle ages."

"People in the middle ages didn't camp under inflatable plastic rafts with the characters from *Friends* on it."

"It was either that or *Barbie*. Do we have any rope or not?"

"No, but I know where we can get some."


It took Geoffrey an hour to blow up the inflatable raft. I refused to help because he made so much spit you could hear it bubbling inside the mouthpiece. He changed into board-shorts and paddled across the river. I watched from my chair as he reached the other side. It was steep but the roots of the gum tree that my father had tied a rope swing to many years before weaved their way down into the water, creating natural steps. Geoffrey pulled the raft up onto a root, balanced it, and made his way up. He stood looking up at the tree for a few minutes then started climbing. He made it all the way up to the branch the rope was tied to, edged his way out and began to untie it. A light breeze caught the raft far below him; it swayed back and forth for a few seconds before sliding gently into the water. The river's current wasn't strong but there was definitely a flow, the raft rotated a few times as it headed off. Geoffrey hadn't noticed so I yelled to him. He was a fair distance away but looked around, waved, and went back to the knot. The rope fell and Geoffrey made his way back down the tree. Gathering the rope up in a loop, he approached the roots to climb down. The raft was well over a hundred feet away, moving quickly now that it had neared the middle of the river. Geoffrey raised his hands and yelled something.

"What?"

"The raft is floating away!"

"I know. Swim out and get it!"

"What?"

"Swim after it!"

"I'm not swimming. I don't know what's in the water."

"You're going to have to swim all the way back if you don't get to it."

"Oh yeah."

Geoffrey lowered himself delicately off the roots into the water, his foot touched something and he jumped back out quickly.

"Is there anything in the river that will bite me?"

"No. Just turtles."

"Do turtles bite?"

"...No. You'd better hurry, the raft's moving pretty quickly."

"I should have worn my shoes."

"Yes, probably."

"Okay. I'm going in. I'm really not happy about this though."

"You'll be fine."

Geoffrey secured the loop of rope around his neck and lowered himself into the water with a few yells of terror. Pushing off, he swam breaststroke towards the raft, keeping his head high above water and looking around nervously. The rope bobbed around his face, obscuring his view and tangling, so he took it off and held one end in his teeth, letting it trail. A fish jumped out of the water a few feet from him, creating a decent splash. Geoffrey screamed and swam faster, the rope discarded. He hadn't gained any distance on the raft and after a few minutes of fear-driven furious dedication, gave up. When I saw that he was abandoning the raft, I yelled, "Swim!" in encouragement but apparently he thought I yelled, "Fin!" which is why he screamed again and hurtled towards the shore as if he was bodysurfing a wave. He was sobbing as he climbed up the bank. The raft floated around the bend and was gone from sight.

"Well that was a fucking waste of time."

"At least you got a turn on the raft."

"What are we going to do now?"

"Go home."

"No, we're not giving up after one small setback. We'll just have to sleep under the stars like they did in the middle ages."

"I thought you said they slept under tarpaulins."

"Some of them. Some of them didn't have tarpaulins. It was hard times. Besides, it's warm and the sky is clear. It'll be nice. We can sleep around the fire. Like knights."

"I'll probably just sleep in the car."

"No you won't. How is that camping together?"

"Laying down in the dirt on the edge of the river isn't really camping."

"Fine, you can sleep in a chair. I'm going to do it properly though."

"There are scorpions around here."

"Are there? I might sleep in a chair as well then. It means I can jump up quicker if we're attacked by dingoes anyway. You should probably make yourself a spear."

We had hotdogs without buns for dinner. Geoffrey had forgotten to re-tie the bag when he grabbed the snack for the pelicans and it was full of ants. We cooked the hotdogs on a stick over the fire, like they did in the middle ages, and they were pretty good. We'd collected enough firewood from the surrounding brush to last the night and even dragged over a big old mallee stump to throw on top after the fire had some decent coals. We sat by the roaring fire drinking beer and watching the cliffs turn from red to orange and pink, then grey as dusk set in. Geoffrey was in full mediaeval armour, his sword across his lap. I'd finally agreed to wear the chapeau à bec, which turned out to be a Robin Hood cap, after Geoffrey complained about group participation. It had cooled as the sun reached the horizon, both of us had our legs in the sleeping bags Geoffrey had borrowed from his nephews; they were children's sleeping bags and only came to our waists. Mine had Buzz Lightyear on it, Geoffrey's was just red with the Ferrari logo. Fish splashed as they fed by the willow and a large egret waded slowly out from the hanging branches. It froze for a moment, then stabbed the water with its long beak, it's prize flashing silver in the last light.

Have you ever done a poo and it was so wet that when you wiped, it was like sticking the paper in a bucket of water?"

"Jesus Christ, Geoffrey. I was enjoying the moment."

"Well excuse me. Just making conversation."

"And you picked your swampy arse as the topic?"

"Well what would you like to talk about?"

"What?"

"Pick a topic."

"We don't need a topic. You're at the river, Geoffrey, relax and enjoy it. Have another beer and talk about river things."

"Like what?"

"Well, when I was kid, I used to jump off those cliffs. We should swim across and do that tomorrow."

"That's not happening. I'm never going back in that water again. It's terrifying."

"You're not going to go swimming at all?"

"No. Something touched my leg out in the deep bit."

"Fine, suit yourself."

"I will."

"Alright."

"Well that wasn't a very good conversation. I'm going to whittle a spoon out of wood."

Geoffrey whittled his spoon and I watched the flames. We both drank a lot of beer. The topics of conversation ranged from ideal spoon depth to whether we'd have sex with a shemale if she looked like Sandra Bullock and we were marooned together on a tropical island. Beyond the light and crackling of the fire, it was pitch black and silent. I put my head back and looked up at the stars. They were the same stars that my father had pointed out and named to me; the Southern Cross, George and Mildred, the Sheep and the Shoe.

I jerked awake in my chair, confused where I was for a moment. It was still dark but there was a hint of dawn approaching. The fire had gone out some time during the night and I was shivering with cold. A wisp of smoke from the ashes indicated that there might still be coals so I achingly leant forward and poked at them with a stick. Geoffrey was nowhere to be seen. He was asleep in the car. With the ignition on auxiliary and the heater running.

"Can we push start it?"

"No, you can't push-start an automatic. I can't believe this, Geoffrey. What the fuck where you thinking?"

"I was cold. And uncomfortable."

"You left me to the cold and uncomfort. Couldn't you have at least put more wood on the fire before you fucked off to your climate-controlled luxury suite?"

"It was still going when I got in the car."

"How were you cold if the fire was still going?"

"I wasn't cold until I got in the car."

"What?"

"I heard a noise."

'What kind of noise?"

"A rustle."

"Is that what knight's in the middle ages did? Heard a rustle and jumped into the nearest automobile?"

"Knights took it in turns to keep watch. They didn't all sleep at the same time. That's how you get stabbed."

"It was probably just a bird."

"No, it was a big rustle. A dingo-sized rustle."

"Right, well it's probably best you sought safety then. I mean, if it *had* been a dingo, there's no point in both of us being torn apart or dragged off into the darkness."

I could see you perfectly out of the window, I had the headlights on. If a dingo attacked you, I would have honked the horn."

"You had the headlights on? Where you listening to the radio as well?"

"No. There's no reception out here so I listened to CDs."

The battery was almost dead; there was barely a click when I turned the ignition. Words were said and then apologised for. A chair was kicked into the water and then retrieved with a sword. We had a lengthy discussion about electrons moving quicker when heated and decided it couldn't hurt to remove the battery and place it near the fire for an hour or so to warm it up but we both knew it was a stretch. The tire wrench didn't fit the bolts holding the battery in place but we managed to pry the clamps off with Geoffrey's sword and set the battery a few feet from the fire pit. I stoked the coals and added a few sticks and the Burger King bag to get it going. Geoffrey cooked the last of the hotdogs over the fire as the sun rose and I boiled a mug of water on the coals to make coffee. I'd bought milk, sugar and a jar of instant coffee in Morgan but forgot to buy water so I used melted ice from the cooler. We tried the battery after a few hours, it was quite warm to the touch but apparently the electrons weren't excited enough to care.

"We're stranded in the Outback. Like those people you hear about on the news that drive out into the Outback unprepared and die and you think, what an idiot, but this time it's us."
"We're not stranded, Geoffrey. Worse case scenario, one of us has to walk out to the main road and hitchhike into Morgan to get a replacement battery."
"It's miles back to main road, you'll never make it."
"What makes you think I'd be the one going? You're the one who drained the battery."

"I don't know the way. I was blindfolded. What's the best case scenario?"

"Well, a boat might cruise past. If we waved them down, they might give us a lift to Morgan... or, if the boat's bigger than just a fishing dinghy with a two-stroke on the back, they might let us use their battery to jump start the car."

"That's definitely the better option. So we just wait?"

"We were planning to stay another night anyway and there's nothing else we can do. I'll probably go for a swim when it warms up a bit."

"No, don't."

"Why not?"

"It's like one of those horror movies where one of them goes swimming and gets pulled under and the other one stands on the bank calling out to them and then goes close to the water and looks down and something grabs him as well."

"Then stay away from the edge if I get pulled under."

"I'd still be out here all alone. How long do you think it will be before a boat goes by?"

"Who knows."

"Should I make an SOS out of rocks on the bank?"

"Sure."

Geoffrey ran out of rocks halfway through the first S so he made it into an arrow instead. He also made a flag to wave by tying the Ferrari sleeping bag to a long branch. We sat by the edge of the river and waited. If this was a movie, there'd be a montage here to show the passing of time; it would include Geoffrey performing a flag dance and throwing it into the air and almost catching it, spear-fishing with his sword in ankle deep water, a game of who can throw a stick closest to the cooler, and three and a half games of charades.

"I give up, Geoffrey"

"Oh, come on. You gave up on the other two. Play this one out."

"Fine. So it's a movie, two words, first word sounds like violin. I have no idea. Do the second word... second word sounds like... finger? No? Ring?"

"Mmhm."

"Okay, second word sounds like ring. Violin ring... I give up, what is it?"

"*The Lion King.* I get to go again."

"*The Lion King* is three words. And violin doesn't sound anything like lion."

"It does if you mumble it."

"Right, I'm not playing anymore."

"Come on, one more go."

"No, it's just painful. I'm going to have another beer and then go for a swim."

"One more while you're having your beer."

"Fine."

"Okay... um... oh, okay, I've got one..."

"Movie."

"Mmhm."

"Two words."

"Mmhm."

"Is it *Those Magnificent Men in Their Flying Machines?*"

We froze. Geoffrey's eyes opened wide and he raised a finger to his lips. The distant but unmistakable noise of an outboard motor grew louder. It was coming from down river and we both ran to the bank and craned our necks to look around the bend. Geoffrey grabbed his flag and began waving it madly as a houseboat came into view. "Help!" he screamed. I waved my arms and yelled, "Hey!" as "Help!" seemed more something you'd yell if you were drowning or being attacked by a dingo - a flat battery lends itself more to, "Excuse me, sorry to trouble you." It looked like there were several people at the front of the houseboat and they were all looking our way. I waved frantically and decided "Help!" was a viable option. The houseboat was directly across from us when I realised it wasn't people; it was the cast from *Friends*. Geoffrey's raft was propped up against a railing and the old lady wearing a pink hat was standing beside it. She gave us the finger as the houseboat passed by.

"What a bitch!"

"I saw that coming as soon as I noticed the pink hat."

"She stole my raft and left us to die."

"We're not going to die. Another boat will come past eventually. I'm going for a swim."

"I might go in too actually. I'm pretty sweaty from waving the flag."

"I thought you were terrified of river monsters pulling you under?"

"At least it would be quick. It's better than slowly starving to death out here."

We swam across to the other side. I did the thing where you scream and go under the water as if something's pulled you under but Geoffrey just glared and kept swimming. To the left of the swinging rope tree, cliffs ran straight into the water but I remembered all the best spots to climb up. There was an old rusty iron pipe that ran all the way from the top of the cliff into the water, which we used to pull ourselves up onto a large smooth boulder. Geoffrey tanned himself like a giant white lizard while I climbed up to a ledge, ten or so feet above, and jumped off. I tried to convince Geoffrey to have a go but he wasn't having any of that and quoted made-up statistics of how many people die jumping off things into water. I climbed back up and jumped off several times. There were higher ledges above me but I hadn't been able to reach them when I was younger. Or perhaps it had just seemed too dangerous to jump from that height and I had never tried. I grabbed onto the iron pipe and lifted myself up; it was a good five feet higher than the first ledge. I'd never been this far up the cliff and it offered a great view. There was another ledge so I made my way up to it. Then another. I looked down, there was no way I was going to jump from this height but I could see far up the river. I climbed another ledge and the area flattened out somewhat. Using the iron pipe as a kind of banister rail, I was able to walk up to the very top from that point. I heard Geoffrey shout, "What are you doing?" from below and I yelled back that I was almost at the top of the cliff and could see for miles. I waited for him to scramble up to join me and we continued to the top together.

"What was at the top?" Seb asked. He was seven and it was his first time at the spot. We were sitting by the edge of the river drinking beer. I'd poured a little bit in a cup for him and he was sipping at it, making a face.

"Orange trees," I answered, "Thousands of orange trees. The iron pipe is an irrigation pipe that supplies an orchard. We walked through the orchard, eating oranges, and after about twenty minutes, came to a house with a big red barn. An old man was inside the barn, fixing his tractor, and we asked if we could use his phone. He called a mechanic in Morgan for us, who piloted his boat down the river and gave us a jump-start. We left that afternoon and this is the first time I've been back since."

"Have I met Geoffrey?"

"When you were a bit younger. He was struck by lightning at a Mediaeval Society event a few years back. Apparently they were out in the woods - probably chasing each other with swords - and ran and huddled together under a tree when a thunderstorm rolled in. A few of them survived, those that weren't wearing chainmail I suppose, but Geoffrey didn't make it. The news did a follow-up interview with one of the survivors a week or so later and her face was just burnt puss - bandages hid most of it but when she talked you could see she had no gums."

"What are you meant to do?"

"Sorry?"

"In a thunderstorm. Are you meant to just stand out in the open? That seems just as dangerous."

"I think you're meant to just lay down flat, so you're not the highest point. I'm not sure though, seems like a strange thing to do - to just lie down on the ground in the open getting wet. I'd probably run under a tree."

"At least he got to see the spot. It's nice out here."

"It is. If I ever make enough money, I'll build a cabin out here. Over the water, with cantilevers."

"What's a cantilever?"

"It's a projecting girder fixed at only one end."

"I like it how it is. Can we swim over to the cliffs and jump off?"

"Sure, after I finish my beer."

The sound of an outboard motor in the distance grew louder and a houseboat cruised around the bend. Seb grinned at me and I nodded.

# Signs

When my wife Holly and I are arguing, I'll double down rather than admit I'm in the wrong. Sometimes I'll triple or quadruple down. It doesn't matter what the argument is about, we once didn't speak for two days because I wouldn't accept that the blonde girl who plays Piper in *Orange is the New Black* wasn't the same girl from the movie *Clueless*.

Just a few months ago, I ordered a pair of expensive pants online. Nowhere in the description did it state they were 'skinny' and the twelve pleats around the crotch weren't noticeable in the photos. When I tried them on, my lower half looked like a pumpkin stuck on two poles. I intended to return them but forgot and missed the thirty-day window. When Holly complained that it was a waste of money, I stated that I actually liked the pants a lot and had changed my mind about returning them. They were, in fact, my favourite pants. I wore them to Olive Garden that night - it was Holly's parent's anniversary and they had a $50 gift card. The left leg seam gave out as I climbed into our booth which was quite disappointing as they were the best pants in the world and really it was Holly's fault for making me decide to wear them that night when I'd actually been saving them for a special occasion. I ordered another pair.

**From**: David Thorne
**Date**: Saturday 19 August 2017 10.07am
**To**: Carl Mishler
**Subject**: Sign

Hello Carl,

Hope you are doing well. I saw an ambulance at your place Thursday night and thought you may have died but I see you've mowed since then.

As you know, we listed our house for sale this week.

Our agent has organized two showings for tomorrow evening and, as such, I was wondering if you'd mind removing the large Trump/Pence sign from your front yard?

It's been several months since Trump won the election and I doubt anybody requires further convincing of what an outstanding choice he was.

Regards, David

..............................................................................................

**From**: Carl Mishler
**Date**: Saturday 19 August 2017 12.29pm
**To**: David Thorne
**Subject**: Re: Sign

I told you not to email again.

**From**: David Thorne
**Date**: Saturday 19 August 2017 12.37pm
**To:** Carl Mishler
**Subject**: Re: Re: Sign

Hello Carl,

I assumed that was only in regard to the HOA fees. And the bonfire. I accepted responsibility for it getting out of hand and offered compensation for your myrtle.

Regards, David.

.........................................................................................

**From**: Carl Mishler
**Date**: Saturday 19 August 2017 6.22pm
**To**: David Thorne
**Subject**: Re: Re: Re: Sign

No its everything. Ive got a right to have a sign in my own yard. And yhy would i know your selling your house? I couldnt care less. Good riddance.

From: David Thorne
Date: Saturday 19 August 2017 6.51pm
To: Carl Mishler
Subject: Re: Re: Re: Re: Sign

Hello Carl,

My mistake. While making coffee this morning, I watched from the kitchen window as you made your way to the realtor's sign in front of our house and took a printed sales sheet from the plastic display unit. The sheets include photos, details and pricing of our property but it's entirely possible you may have mistaken the information for boat-building instructions or a sewing pattern.

I'll address the issue with the realtor - maybe have them add a few starbursts and a photo of a *Dancing With the Stars* contestant.

I understand you have a right to share your political preferences with passing vehicles and I'm not asking you to remove the Trump/Pence sign permanently. In fact, putting it back up after we've sold the house will save the new owners months of wondering if they made the right decision.

Regards, David.

**From**: Carl Mishler
**Date**: Sunday 20 August 2017 8.43am
**To**: David Thorne
**Subject**: Re: Re: Re: Re: Re: Sign

Myabe you shoudl find something better to do than spying on people. Im not taking down my sign. Why would i do you any favors? You dont respect the property lines and you let your dogs run wild and smoke pot. nobody wants you here. theres been 4 complaints at the HOA meetings about you riding ATVs on the street. Probably when your high. We had a friendly village atmopsphere before you moved here.

......................................................................................................................

**From**: David Thorne
**Date**: Sunday 20 August 2017 9.25am
**To**: Carl Mishler
**Subject**: Re: Re: Re: Re: Re: Re: Sign

Carl,

Firstly, our dogs don't smoke pot. Laika just isn't into it and Banksy will lose his forklift license if he tests positive at work.

Secondly, it's a subdivision, Carl, not a village - you're the subdivision idiot. Nobody wants to live in a village. I've seen them in movies, there's pigs and goats everywhere and everyone has to run when the king's swordsmen ride through. Our letterbox is at the entry to the subdivision which is too far to walk and too close to drive so I take the ATV. At least it gives you something to discuss at the meetings apart from how much you all love Consumer Cellular.

I simply assumed you'd begrudgingly facilitate a simple request that may increase the likelihood of us no longer being neighbors. It's not as if I asked you to remove the plastic wishing-well with the huge $39.95 Dollar General store sticker - or the cast-iron single bed frame you turned into a flowerbed on your front lawn - it looks like a child's grave, Carl. Nobody is driving past your house and declaring to their passengers, "Oh look, that's a creative use of a child's bed, the owner must be a professional landscape designer, let's stop and make a wish." They're shuddering and locking the doors.

Would you consider covering the sign with a tarp?

Regards, David.

..................................................................................................................

**From**: Carl Mishler
**Date**: Sunday 20 August 2017 3.02pm
**To**: David Thorne
**Subject**: Re: Re: Re: Re: Re: Re: Re: Sign

Kiss my ass. Im not covering it with anything. Ive got a right have a sign on my own property and Im proud of our president. Trumps done more for this country already than obama ever did and lying hillary ever would.

·················································································

**From**: David Thorne
**Date**: Sunday 20 August 2017 3.49pm
**To**: Carl Mishler
**Subject**: Re: Re: Re: Re: Re: Re: Re: Re: Sign

Carl,

I never stated otherwise. Suggesting, as some may, that Trump is anything other than a man of integrity, empathy and intelligence, shows little faith, if not contempt, in the judgment and values of the people who voted for him. Nobody would purposely elect an uneducated narcissistic sociopath to represent the people of the United States... to say, "This is our best. This is who we are." It would just be embarrassing.

Rather than bickering, we should all sit down together, perhaps over a plate of ramp & squirrel pie with grits at your place, and discuss what we are going to do with the shit-ton of coal we're all going to have once the mines are opened again. My suggestion, for what it's worth, is to pile it up along the Mexican border and set it alight. Rounding up and forcing the LGBT community, atheists, Muslims, non-whites, the unemployed and baby murderers to work in the mines would free up millions of real jobs.

Angry Bob from Hazard, Kentucky can finally move out of his doublewide and take that management position at a H&M in Seattle he's always longed for.

I wasn't questioning your right to display a sign and I do understand your reluctance to remove it, it's a double down thing: A Clinton landslide was predicted and the 'libtards' gloated so it was perfectly reasonable for you to gloat in November. Sure, Trump's played a bit of golf since then and each and every promise has been abandoned, diluted, or blocked by the courts or his own party, but this, of course, is entirely the fault of biased liberal media. We'd all be living in solid gold RVs and eating out at Denny's every night by now if they'd just let him do his job... Admitting, "Fuck, we elected an absolute dickhead, sorry about that," simply isn't an option because it's still your turn to gloat goddamnit.

Regards, David

···········································································································

**From**: Carl Mishler
**Date**: Monday 21 August 2017 11.40am
**To**: David Thorne
**Subject**: Re: Re: Re: Re: Re: Re: Re: Re: Re: Sign

Boo hoo Im sad because Trump won. Get over it snowflake. This used to be a great country and its going to be again. the signs staying up. End of conversation. And keep your fucking dogs out of my yard. Im going to throw a party when you leave.

**From:** David Thorne
**Date:** Monday 21 August 2017 12.18pm
**To:** Carl Mishler
**Subject:** Re: Re: Re: Re: Re: Re: Re: Re: Re: Re: Sign

Carl,

I've lived here three years and the only person I've ever seen visit you is the guy who fixed your lawnmower last year. Is the party just going to be you and Jim from Jim's Mower & Backhoe Repairs standing around admiring each other's red hat and reminiscing about when, for a dime, you could take your sweetie to the matinee and buy sodas at the drug store afterwards - possibly with enough left over for a funnel-cake to share at the local park during that evening's negro hanging?

Regardless, you'll be pleased to learn we received and accepted an offer on our property this morning. I'm sure you'll get along well with the buyers - Mike & Taylor and their two miniature frenchies. Mike's an instructor at Planet Fitness and Taylor runs a small calligraphy business from home so if you'd like hand-written invites for the party or your next clan tractor-pull & pig-lingerie swap-meet, he's your man.

Regards, David.

**From**: Carl Mishler
**Date**: Monday 21 August 2017 1.54pm
**To**: David Thorne
**Subject**: Re: Re: Re: Re: Re: Re: Re: Re: Re: Re: Re: Sign

MAKE AMERICA GREAT AGAIN

# Cantilevers

My Design History lecturer at uni, Mr Bruton, had a very monotonous voice. It was as if a robot was reading one very long sentence. There was no inflection, no emphasis, no apparent excitement for the subject. Except when he spoke of Frank Lloyd Wright's, *Fallingwater*.

Mr Bruton's voice came alive when he spoke of *Fallingwater*, his body became animated and he thrashed his arms about wildly as he described its integration with the natural surroundings, it's bold cantilevered balconies, the ledge rock protruding through the living room to demonstrably link the outside with the inside. Then, just as quickly, he'd become angry. Angry at those in the lecture theatre with their heads down on folded arms, those who were looking at their laptops, those talking. He'd yell that to be uninterested in something so visionary, so beautiful, so 'designed', meant an inability to grasp the fundamental principles of design. As it was a design course with limited enrollment spots and hundreds of applicants each year, it meant those not embracing the principles of design had no right to be there and had robbed the spot of someone more worthy. They were 'Spot Robbers'. Occasionally a Spot Robber argued back that they were there to learn about graphic design, not old buildings, but they only ever did so once. Mr Bruton once threw a lamp across the room and kicked over a lectern before storming out screaming, "Fail. You all fail. Join the Army or get a job in retail because you'll never be real designers." Anger requires passion and nobody was more passionate about *Fallingwater* than Mr Bruton.

I thought *Fallingwater* looked like it had been designed in five minutes by a child with building blocks.

As part of our course structure, we had a class called *Designer/Client Relationships,* which really should have been titled *Can I See It In a Different Colour?* The class basically consisted of us being given a design brief, which we would fulfill, and then the lecturer, acting as the client, would tell us he hated it. It was meant to teach compromise, to accept a balance between creativity and the client's needs, that an elaborate four colour corporate identity with transparencies and a spot-varnish means nothing to a client who sells shoes, wants a shoe as his logo, can only afford to print in one colour, and needs it by tomorrow. Also the logo is mainly going to be used on faxes.

"What's this?"
"It's a graphic representation of two swans with their necks wrapped around each other's. The swans symbolise partnership and the negative space between the necks forms a leaf shape representing growth and the company's commitment to renewable resources."
"We sell toasters."

Frank Lloyd Wright never took a course in Designer/Client Relationships.

"Thanks for meeting us on site, Frank."

"No problem, Edgar."

"What we're looking for is a small holiday cabin about fifty-feet from the river."

"Gotcha, *on* the river."

"No, fifty-feet from the edge. So we can see the river and waterfall while we're relaxing on the patio."

"You'd still be able to see the river if I built the house on it, you'd just have to stand up and look down over the balcony."

"That doesn't sound very practical. I'd like to be able to see the river while I'm sitting down."

"I could add a glass floor bit for you to look through."

"That's hardly the same as being able to see the whole river, is it? We'd just see water running underneath. What about the waterfall?"

"It's not that great. I've seen bigger ones. Besides, if you're over the waterfall, you'll be able to hear it better."

"I'm just not sure it's..."

"Right, you know what? I don't think I want to build it at all anymore."

"Don't be like that, Frank. Fine, we'll discuss the location of the house later and maybe come up with some kind of compromise."

"No, I'm going home. There's heaps of other projects I'd much rather be working on."

"Okay, you can build it on the river."

"Really?"

"Yes. Now, for the materials, we were thinking either cedar or redwood."

"Gotcha, twelve-thousand tons of cantilevered reinforced concrete."

"Sorry?"

"Nothing."

"We want it in either cedar or redwood, Frank."

"Sure. So what's your budget for this project?"

"Thirty-five thousand*."

"Okay, so somewhere between thirty-five thousand and two-hundred thousand. I can work with that. Oh, by the way, how do you feel about really low ceilings?"

"We'd like really grand ceilings, at least twelve-feet."

"Got it."


Apparently Frank was a bit of dick outside of work as well. Ignoring 'accepted rules of conduct' of the time, he walked out on his wife and six children, leaving them destitute, and moved in with a client's wife. This well-publicized affair ended when a pissed off butler slaughtered Frank's mistress and six others with an axe. One of Frank's relatives described him as, "an embarrassment" and "a torment" to the family."

---

* *Thirty-five thousand dollars was a lot of money in the 1930s. The average cost of a home was seven-thousand and the average yearly income was only twelve-hundred. My neighbour Carl bought his very first lawnmower in 1932 for eleven cents. He still has photos of it and and brings them out sometimes to show people at the supermarket.*

We forgive Frank for his ego and conduct though, given his extraordinary contribution to the world. It's how everyone in the design industry justifies their own dreadful behaviour. I've never met a designer who didn't think they were the most creative human being to have ever lived, and therefore can get away with acting like a petulant child. Except myself of course.

The design course I was in had six subjects but the Design History component of the course was worth 25% of our grade. Two other subjects, Design Principles and Design Technologies, were pass or fail. There was no end-of-year test for Design History but, rather, a dissertation which consisted of each student giving a ten minute presentation on an iconic design or designer of their choice - to the entire lecture theatre.

I'm not a fan of public speaking. I've experienced social anxiety, in varying degrees, all my life. Sometimes I'm fine, sometimes I won't leave the house for weeks. Not even to visit friends. It makes no sense and I realise it's irrational but there are days when even the thought of interacting with other people causes a mild panic attack and I break out in a sweat. Once at uni, I was walking across a bridge between two buildings and a girl I knew stopped to say hello so I ran. There was no logic to my action, I simply stared at her in horror for a second, then bolted. My worst fear is being in one those groups where you're all sitting around in a circle and the group leader says, "Okay, we'll go around the circle and have each person tell us their name and something about themselves."

Apparently the only way to overcome social anxiety is to join an 'active behavioural therapy group' which includes sitting around in a circle talking about yourself.

"Oh, you're scared of spiders?"
"Yes, terrified."
"Me too. You should join the therapy group I'm in."
"Will it fix my phobia?"
"No, we just sit around in a circle and the group leader throws spiders at us. Big hairy ones. It's dreadful."

I've gotten better at social interaction over the years, and at times worse, but back then, presenting a Design History dissertation to an entire class was the worst thing I could imagine... which was made worse when, two weeks before we were to present to the class, Mr Bruton singled me out as a Spot Robber.

"David."
"Shhh, he's talking about cantilevers again."
"What are you doing your dissertation on?"
"I don't know yet. What are you doing yours on?"
"Charles and Ray Eames."
"Nice. I like their chairs."
"You haven't started yet? You only have a few weeks."
"I know, every time I think about it, I break out in a sweat and have to do deep-breathing exercises."

"David and Jamie, am I boring you?"

"No, not at all. Sorry Mr Bruton, I was just agreeing with your point about cantilevers."

"Oh, really, David?"

"Yes. I find cantilevers very interesting."

"What exactly do you find most interesting about them?"

"The whole process really."

"What process?"

"The process of... levering the canti."

"Do you know how many people applied for this course and didn't get in, David?"

"Eight-hundred and thirty-six."

"Correct, eight-hundred and thirty-six people wanted to sit in the chair you're currently occupying. One of which didn't receive a letter of acceptance because you robbed the spot from them. You're a Spot Robber."

"No, honestly, I'm not a Spot Robber. I'm genuinely interested in the subject. Please continue."

"What are you doing your dissertation on, David?"

"Sorry?"

"Your dissertation."

"I'd rather not say at this time... it would ruin the, um, surprise."

"Oh, it's a surprise is it? How fun. It must be a truly exceptional presentation if you're bound to such secrecy. Maybe I should arrange a video camera on the day to capture the moment for future generations to enjoy and learn from."

"That's probably not necessary."

"It better be worth the wait, David."

I didn't panic for the first week; I told myself two weeks was plenty of time to come up with something. It was a comforting lie so I embraced it. When I had a week until the presentation, I told myself a week was plenty of time, then five days was plenty, then four... With two days left, I deliberated faking an injury, maybe hiring a wheelchair and wheeling into Mr Bruton's office wearing a neck brace and explaining, by writing on a notepad, that my throat was crushed in a terrible accident. I probably wouldn't need the wheelchair for that actually.

I was capable of forging a doctor's certificate if the need arose. I'd done it before. I had a decent computer setup at home by 90s standards - a Macintosh IIfx with a large monitor and scanner - and it wasn't difficult to scan a certificate in and edit it in Photoshop. It would only mean an extension on my dissertation though; I wouldn't be getting out of it. I had the choice of either failing the subject or speaking in front of an audience.

A friend named Geoffrey had introduced me to Macintosh systems a few years before when we'd both worked at a printing firm together. He became a certified Apple technician around the same time I was accepted into uni and worked at a store called Next Byte for a while which gave him access to a lot of software. Most of my pirated copies came from him back then as this was before even Limewire existed. We spent hundreds of hours, possibly thousands, looking at new programs while smoking dope and listening to music in his apartment. Most of the music Geoffrey listened to was classical but occasionally he'd let me sneak in a bit of Pop Will Eat Itself or Sisters of Mercy to the playlist with only a small amount of complaining about the lack of structure, balance or beauty.

I put on earphones and listened to music, leaning back in my chair and staring at a blank page on the monitor in front of me. Reaching for a book on design history, from a large stack I had borrowed from the uni library that morning, I flicked through, put it down and picked up another. I'd already done this several times, it was like opening the fridge to see if there's anything to eat, then checking again five minutes later with lowered expectations. I glanced back up at the monitor, a screen-saver had kicked in. It showed beach scenes, fading from one image to another with a slow zoom. I watched it for a few minutes, nodding my head to the music. The bass line synchronised with the images as if they were made for one another.

"Geoffrey. It's David."
"What's up?"
"What's that fade called on screen-savers? The one where it zooms and fades in and out of images."
"The Ken Burns effect?"
"That's the one, do you have software that does that? Maybe one that syncs to music?"
"Sure."
"What are you up to at the moment?"

"Listening to Vivaldi while I polish my sword."

"Nice. Do you mind if I drop by?"

"Sure, bring some floppies. I've worked out how to turn 720k floppies into 1.44mb ones just by drilling a hole in the top left edge."

Jamie finished his dissertation. Halfway through he'd lost his place and stammered a little but it was well written and covered the subject adequately. There was polite clapping from the audience and Mr Bruton nodded.

"Thank you, Jamie. That was very good. I would have liked to hear more about the relationship between Charles and Ray Eames and Herman Miller but a well rounded presentation nonetheless. Next up, we have... oh, good, David and his secret surprise. He's even bought in his computer and arranged a projector. We're all in a for special treat today. David?"

I made my way down to the podium where I'd set up my computer earlier. I didn't own a laptop in those days so I'd taken in my entire system, which included a decent amp and speakers. Someone had tripped over one of the speaker wires earlier so I plugged it back in and cranked the volume to max. A low hum filled the lecture theatre. I mirrored my screen to the projector, asked for the lights to be turned off, and double-clicked a file titled, *One_thousand_words.mov*

The opening of Vivaldi's *Winter* from *Four Seasons* flooded the dark room. River rocks and rhododendrons appeared on the screen, then blueprints from Frank Lloyd Wrights *Fallingwater*, the images merging into another seamlessly thanks to Ken Burns, synchronised to the music. At what was probably the 1700s orchestral equivalent of a 'drop', the blueprints were replaced by images of the house. There were over two-hundred images in all, it had taken hours to scan them all. They showed exteriors, and a few interiors, of the house in winter, spring, summer & autumn and matched the edited relative compositions from *Four Seasons* - timed to be exactly ten minutes.

I had no idea how it was going to be received. It was a risky move but a move that meant I didn't have to speak. I half expected Mr Bruton, at any moment, to turn on the lights mid-presentation and ask, "Is this meant to be some kind of joke?" but somehow, I didn't care. Something had occurred while I was constructing the presentation. It began as an out, a way to avoid having to do a real dissertation, but as I selected images and timed their appearance to the music, details in the architecture stood out. Window panes went straight into the rock rather than having frames, balconies floated as if defying gravity - metal, concrete and glass merged seamlessly into the natural environment like it belonged there... needed to be there. Juxtaposing forms which I'd previously seen as children's building blocks were actually structured like a grid. A *perfect* grid, regardless of angle, distance or detail of the photos.

The presentation ended on a long violin note and a hero shot of the house surrounded by autumnal leaves before fading out. I heard someone trip on a step and fumble with the light switch and the room was suddenly very bright. Jamie clapped and a few others joined in but not overly enthusiastically. I looked across the room to where Mr Bruton was sitting, expecting to see him shaking his head with disdain, or worse, smirking. He was wiping an eye with his tie.

"That was beautiful. Thank you, David."
"Are you being sarcastic?"
"Not at all. I'd actually like a copy."
"I can never tell when you're being sarcastic."
"I'm not being sarcastic."
"Does this mean I pass?"
"I'll give you a distinction if you can tell me what a cantilever is."
"It's a projecting girder fixed at only one end, it's how Wright managed to create balconies that look like they're defying gravity."
"Very good. Next up is... Jodie."
"Fuck."
"Language, Jodie."

Holly and I held hands as we walked along a path bordered by tall native rhododendrons. It was twenty years since I had graduated, a few years since I had moved to the United States to live. We were with a group consisting of only seven or eight people as we had booked the first morning tour months ahead. It had been a dry summer and the leaves were turning late but there were hints of orange and red as our tour guide led us along the winding path. The foliage blocked sight of the house right up until we rounded a final corner. Holly squeezed my hand hard and smiled.

"Oh my god, David, are you crying?"
"No, my eyes just went a bit moist."
"It's beautiful."
"Yes, it is."
"The balconies look like they're floating."
"Cantilevers."

# Watching Jeopardy With People Who Are Going Deaf

**Alex Trebek:** "Botanically, a peanut isn't a nut but one of these, like a soybean."

**Me:** "Legume."

**Holly's father:** "Legume."

**Me:** Throws hands up as if to say, "What the fuck?"

**Contestant:** What is a legume."

**Alex Trebek:** "Correct."

**Holly's father:** Nods head wisely.

Repeat.

# Ben's Car

My car interior gets a little messy sometimes, everyone's does. Generally, when a vehicle is first purchased, it's cleaned out religiously for a few months, then intermittently, then when the console gets a bit cluttered with candy wrappers, receipts, lighters and notes. I smoke in my car so my cleaning schedule is based on how full the ashtray gets but if I have to pick someone up on short notice, I'll do the equivalent of hiding dirty dishes in the cupboard when people give you five minutes warning that they're coming over and shove the candy wrappers, receipts, lighters and notes in the glove box or center console, maybe give the dashboard a quick wipe with my sleeve.

This is not the case with my coworker Ben's car. Ben drives a blue 2006 Toyota Camry that last had the interior cleaned, I'm assuming, in 2006. An archaeological excavation of the layers is probably the only way to determine for sure but once, when he picked me up from the airport, I had to burrow with my feet to make room in the front passenger footwell and found a dead mouse - flattened like a pressed flower in a dictionary. It probably made its way in to feast on remnants of takeaway food and couldn't find its way out - or settled in and lived like a king on McDonald's fries and Taco Bell burritos until dying of old age. The rear of the vehicle is worse as you can only see the headrests of the back seats poking out. It's impossible to describe the smell, as it's all of them.

Yesterday, while Ben was in meetings all day and I was procrastinating about laying out a sales brochure for window awnings, I decided to take the keys from Ben's desk and perform a 'stock take' of his vehicle. I made Walter, a junior designer at the agency, do the actual work as I didn't want to touch anything but I gave him a pair of yellow dishwashing gloves from the kitchen to use so the complaining was unwarranted. Also, you'd assume Ben would have been pleased about it (two large garbage bags of rubbish were removed and items that might not have been rubbish were put in archive boxes and placed in his trunk) but he's been going on about 'invasion of privacy' for hours now and is threatening to file a formal complaint.

Regardless, here's a complete list of the contents of Ben's car:

16 McDonald's bags and 9 Burger King bags.
28 empty drink containers.
8 pairs of sunglasses.
12 various charging cables.
6 empty chip packets (barbecue).
2 empty Pringle's cans (sour cream & onion).
16 lighters.
11 unpaid parking tickets.
34 empty cigarette packets (Virginia Slims, Menthol).

760 cigarette butts (approximation).

2 Redbox DVDs (*Battleship* & *The Twilight Saga: Breaking Dawn Part 2*).

38 various takeaway food receipts.

1 sock.

8 scratch'n'win lottery tickets (scratched, no winners).

6 batteries (4 AAA and 2 AA, charge level unknown).

6 baby mice (flat).

3 empty pizza boxes.

1 piece of string (approximately 5" in length).

1 bird's nest.

46 compact disks.

1 panini-maker box containing a pair of boardshorts.

26 used napkins.

1 pair of tongs.

15 pens.

1 laser pen (confiscated).

1 Subway foot-long sandwich (contents unknown, petrified).

1 Fleshlight.

1 Wonderwave Fleshlight replacement sleeve.

1 box of kitchen backsplash tiles.

1 small notepad (green, contains handwritten poetry).

1 copy of Orson Scott Card's *Ender's Game*.

1 plastic sandwich bag containing marijuana (confiscated).

1 Stormtrooper figurine (4", confiscated).

4 unopened reams of A4 paper (suspiciously the same brand we have in the stationary cupboard).

And, finally, 1 box of Betty Crocker Super Moist instant cake mix (unopened, chocolate, expired in 2012).

# Ben's Poetry

I'm not a huge fan of poetry. I'll accept the argument that it's an art form - being an expression of the imagination - but by that broad definition, so are Etch-A-Sketch drawings and Magic Aqua Sand sculptures. I don't think anyone really likes poetry, apart from the ones writing it, and they only really like their own. People declare they like poetry but if pressed to name their favourite poem it's generally a struggle;

"Oh, um, probably *The Road Less Travelled*. It's a classic."
"The 1978 book of psychology and spirituality by M. Scott Peck?"
"No, the poem version. I had to read it in school. It's about a guy who's taking a walk and chooses an overgrown path. It's a metaphor for not worrying about ticks."
"Do you mean *The Road Not Taken*?"
"No, that's a movie about a dad and his son who have to escape from cannibals after the apocalypse. I think Liam Neeson was in it."

I copied and pasted the above text from one of my previous books because, quite honestly, I couldn't be bothered writing a new paragraph about poetry. I've never read a poem and thought, 'that was wonderful, I shall read another' and, if someone recites a poem to me, it's as if my brain is hard-wired to blank out and I just hear a 'womwomwom' noise and see static. Kind of like that girl in the movie *Serenity* when she sees the octopus animation but without the mad fighting skills. Kind of the opposite really. This all changed when I found Ben's small green notepad of handwritten poetry in the back of his car and read every single page. Mostly with horror and a slight tinge of guilt but that's not the point. From what I could work out, much of it is regarding his ex, Sarah, who's either schizophrenic or a twin, is having engine trouble, showers a lot, and cheated with someone named Robert:

## Texts

You said you were at your sister's house,
I knew it wasn't true.
I read his texts while you were showering,
hope you enjoyed the rendezvous.

## Sarah

The engine light won't say what's wrong,
no clue to what it's about.
It just tells you there's a problem,
It's up to you to figure it out.

## Mirror

I could always tell you both apart, it wasn't hard to do.
One was always nice.
The other one was you.

## Cut

The Band-Aid eventually fell off in the shower,
it barely showed a scar.
A blunt knife slips without warning,
like you in Robert's car.

## Bathroom

I threw out your apricot face scrub,
your coconut body wash and apple shampoo.
I bleached the tiles and wiped the sink,
but the bathroom still smells like you.


Personally, I feel the above poem would have made a lot more sense if Ben had ended it with, "but the bathroom still smells like fruit," but what do I know.

Ben does make a valid point about blunt knives though, it's important to keep your kitchen knives sharpened, as a blunt knife is far more dangerous than a sharp one. I recently purchased ten expensive Wüsthof knives, as I've always wanted a set. Last week, Holly and I went away for a few days and her parents stayed at our house to look after the dogs. When we got back, two of the knives were missing and one looked like it had been used to cut concrete. Apparently the missing two fell into the insinkerator, which was then switched on, and the other was used to scrape the barbecue grill clean. Which brings me to:

# Asking Holly's Parents to Housesit While We're Away

I'll open this paragraph by stating that I do appreciate everything Holly's parents do for us. Only because it would have been rude to simply dive straight into details about how they destroy everything while housesitting though. Holly's father recently read one of my books, which contained a few satirical exaggerations about having Thanksgiving dinner at his house, and he didn't speak to me for a month because I'd referred to his baked celery bread balls (with flour and milk sauce) as 'dryballs'.

"How are you, Tom?"

"Hm."

"You're not still cross about the book are you?"

"No, I couldn't give a fuck."

"Good. It was just satirical exagger..."

"It was shit."

"...yes, referring to your baked celery and bread balls as dryballs was certainly a bit uncalled fo..."

"No, the whole book was shit."

"...right, well, they *were* pretty dry."

"That's what the sauce is for you fucking idiot."

Tom is retired US Army and was stationed in Germany for many years which is where he met Maria, Holly's mother. Maria is probably too young to have been a member of the Hitler Youth but based on her unquestioning devotion to the current sociopathic halfwit in the Oval Office, she'd have fit in quite well. She'd have had the most patches, the first to point out dissidents to officials and, had Facebook been around in that era, posted 'Share if you're proud of the Führer' memes eighteen times a day. It's good to have a hobby though.

I'm not sure what hobbies Tom has, if any, but I know he watches a lot of sport on television because when he housesits, he records about 90,000 terabytes of baseball, Nascar and football events onto the cable-box. It takes me around four days to scroll through and delete them all and we're downgraded to dial-up speeds for the remainder of the month.

Last month, after Holly and I arrived home from three days away with our friends JM and Lori, I noticed there was something different about our living room but couldn't quite put my finger on it. The room seemed bigger somehow but contained the same leather sofa and loveseat, the same Noguchi coffee table, the same floor lamp and the same new rug... It wasn't until I sat down and my knees bumped against the coffee table that I realized the rug was half the size it had been before we left and that the furniture had all been pushed closer together to fit on it.

"Hello Tom, it's David. I just noticed the rug and I was wondering what..."

"What rug?"

"The rug in our living room. It's half the size it was."

"Bullshit. It might be a bit smaller but not half."

"Why is it *any* smaller?"

"How the fuck would I know? Maybe it shrank in the dryer."

"You put it in the dryer?"

"I had to wash and dry it. You can't spot-clean lasagna out."

"You dropped lasagna on our new rug?"

"The baking-dish was too hot to carry and I couldn't make it to the dining table in time."

"It was a whole lasagna? Why didn't you use oven-mitts?"

"Why is your dining table so far away from the kitchen?"

"Yes, valid point. When we were laying out the furniture, I should have taken the distance you're capable of carrying a piping hot dish of lasagna with your bare hands into account. Perhaps we should have some kind of lasagna conveyer belt system installed to prevent such a situation happening again."

"There's no reason to be sarcastic about it."

"No, I suppose not. I should probably just be happy it was only lasagna you were throwing about and not a chainsaw or bucket of acid."

"Now you're just being stupid. I'll buy you a new rug if you're going to cry about it. How much was it?"

"Twelve-hundred dollars, it's handcrafted wool."

"That's ridiculous. Home Depot has rugs for $99 and they're a lot nicer than yours. I'll get you one today."

"I don't want a rug from Home Depot."

"They have modern looking ones."

"I've seen them. I wouldn't put one in a crack-house."

"I'll pick out one with a nice pattern."

"It's not going in our house."

"I'm hanging up now."

"Tom, don't buy us a rug from Home Dep... Tom?"

I was wrong about the rug; it would have been quite appropriate in a crack-house. When I was growing up, my parents had bedroom curtains with almost the same exact design - green and blue overlapping circles on an orange background. If you stared at them for too long, you'd get dizzy. They'd had the curtains for as long as I remember and only replaced them when they melted from being too close to an electric heater - so also the same material as the rug.

"Are you sure it isn't an outside rug, Tom? It's very shiny."

"It's an inside/outside rug. You can use it anywhere. Pretty good for forty-five dollars, hey?"

"I thought you said they were ninety-nine?"

"They are, usually, this one was in the sale bin - fifty percent off. With the extra money, I got you a floor lamp."

"We have an Arco floor lamp. It's a design icon."

"This one's a lot nicer, its shade has tassels. Besides, yours doesn't work. It fell over when I was moving the furniture. You're lucky it didn't smash the glass coffee table. Come and help me get it out of the car, I've got a framed print of a steamship in there for you as well."

# Watching the Movie Dante's Peak With Seb

"There's no way that pickup truck would be able to outrun a pyroclastic cloud."

"Oh my god, Seb, I don't talk all the way through movies that you want to watch."

"Yes you do, you complain non-stop. I'm going to look up how fast a pyroclastic cloud travels…"

"Just let me watch the fucking movie."

"… A pyroclastic cloud travels 450 miles per hour."

"I don't care, stop saying pyroclastic cloud. Besides, it may leave the volcano at 450 miles per hour but it would slow down as it gets further away."

"They're right next to the volcano."

"No they're not, Seb. They've been driving for ages. They just passed through a town."

"Yes, at 450 miles per hour apparently. It's probably some kind of land speed record. I'm looking it up…"

"They're not going 450 miles per hour. Look the pyroclastic cloud is catching up to them."

"763 miles per hour is the land speed record. At Black Rock Desert in a car with two Rolls Royce jet engines. Is that Sarah Conner?"

"What? Yes, but you're making me miss bits. I have no idea how they ended up in the mineshaft now. I'll have to rewind it…"

"They drove in and crashed to escape the pyroclastic cloud. And they'd be dead if they crashed going 450 miles per hour. You know what we should do?"

"Shut the fuck up and watch the movie?"

"No, stick *three* Rolls Royce jet engines on a car and break the land speed record. We could stick them on that pickup truck as it's already pretty zippy."

# Prevaricate Pseudologia

**From**: Craig Buchanan
**Date**: Tuesday 14 March 2017 9.32am
**To**: David Thorne
**Subject**: Annual report files

Good morning,

Attached hi-res photos for Unilever AR you asked for.

Also, FYI, Walter was here for an interview yesterday afternoon. I saw him in Jason's office. He applied for the junior designer position we advertised in February. Trouble in paradise?

Craig

....................................................................................

**From**: David Thorne
**Date**: Tuesday 14 March 2017 9.41am
**To**: Craig Buchanan
**Subject**: Re: Annual report files

Nice. He told me he was taking his dog to the vet. Thank you for the files. And the heads up.

David

**From**: David Thorne
**Date**: Tuesday 14 March 2017 9.46am
**To**: Walter Bowers
**Subject**: Vet

Morning Walter,

I hope everything went well at the vet's office yesterday. How's Charlie doing?

David

......................................................................................

**From**: Walter Bowers
**Date**: Tuesday 14 March 2017 9.58am
**To**: David Thorne
**Subject**: Re: Vet

He's ok thanks for asking. just got to take dog antibiotics for a few weeks. The vet said it was probably just a virus.

......................................................................................

**From**: David Thorne
**Date**: Tuesday 14 March 2017 10.05am
**To**: Walter Bowers
**Subject**: Re: Re: Vet

Walter,

Are you confident with the diagnosis? Someone told me recently that their dog was taking antibiotics for a virus but it turned out to be Prevaricate Pseudologia. I think you catch it from ticks. Did they test Charlie for that?

David

·····························································································

**From**: Walter Bowers
**Date**: Tuesday 14 March 2017 10.12am
**To**: David Thorne
**Subject**: Re: Re: Re: Vet

I think so. they did lots of tests and said it was just a virus.

·····························································································

**From**: David Thorne
**Date**: Tuesday 14 March 2017 10.21am
**To**: Walter Bowers
**Subject**: Re: Re: Re: Re: Vet

Walter,

It probably wouldn't hurt to make sure. Even a minor case of Prevaricate Pseudologia can get out of hand before you know it. One moment you're happily digging holes under fences, perhaps to get to greener grass, and the next, covered in tick bites and growling at hobos under a bridge when they try to take your blanket.

Which vet did you take Charlie to?

David

**From:** Walter Bowers
**Date:** Tuesday 14 March 2017 10.26am
**To:** David Thorne
**Subject:** Re: Re: Re: Re: Re: Vet

Just the vet near our place.

........................................................................................

**From:** David Thorne
**Date:** Tuesday 14 March 2017 10.30am
**To:** Walter Bowers
**Subject:** Re: Re: Re: Re: Re: Re: Vet

Walter,

What's the name of it?

David

........................................................................................

**From:** Walter Bowers
**Date:** Tuesday 14 March 2017 10.39am
**To:** David Thorne
**Subject:** Re: Re: Re: Re: Re: Re: Re: Vet

Its just called the veterinary clinic. why? the one on port road near the supermarket.

**From**: David Thorne
**Date**: Tuesday 14 March 2017 10.46am
**To**: Walter Bowers
**Subject**: Re: Re: Re: Re: Re: Re: Re: Re: Vet

Walter,

I'm quite familiar with that vet's office; it's where we take Banksy and Laika. Was it Doctor Wang or Doctor Richard who saw Charlie? Doctor Wang is young and new to the practice so it's possible she may not have the experience to recognise the tell-tale signs of Prevaricate Pseudologia.

David

........................................................................................................

**From**: Walter Bowers
**Date**: Tuesday 14 March 2017 10.58am
**To**: David Thorne
**Subject**: Re: Re: Re: Re: Re: Re: Re: Re: Re: Vet

doctor Richard.

........................................................................................................

**From**: David Thorne
**Date**: Tuesday 14 March 2017 11.06am
**To**: Walter Bowers
**Subject**: Re: Re: Re: Re: Re: Re: Re: Re: Re: Re: Vet

Walter,

You should be fine with the antibiotics then, Doctor Richard knows what he's doing. His stature in the field of veterinary medicine is inversely proportionate to that of his height. Was it odd having a vet who is a dwarf?

David.

---

**From**: Walter Bowers
**Date**: Tuesday 14 March 2017 11.18am
**To**: David Thorne
**Subject**: Re: Re: Re: Re: Re: Re: Re: Re: Re: Re: Re: Vet

no because I'm not predjajuiced.

---

**From**: David Thorne
**Date**: Tuesday 14 March 2017 11.29am
**To**: Walter Bowers
**Subject**: Re: Re: Re: Re: Re: Re: Re: Re: Re: Re: Re: Re: Vet

Walter,

I wasn't inferring you were - it's just that Doctor Richard's dimensions, and his attire, can come as a bit of a surprise if you're not expecting a three-foot tall cross-dressing vet - or three-foot-six if he's in high heels.

Was he wearing high heels, Walter?

David.

**From:** Walter Bowers
**Date:** Tuesday 14 March 2017 11.34am
**To:** David Thorne
**Subject:** Re: Re: Re: Re: Re: Re: Re: Re: Re: Re: Re: Re: Re: Vet

how would I know he was on the other side of the bench that they put the animals on. whats your point?

........................................................................................................

**From:** David Thorne
**Date:** Tuesday 14 March 2017 11.47am
**To:** Walter Bowers
**Subject:** ally?

Walter,

I wasn't making one. The efficiency of a point depends entirely on it not being one the recipient wishes to avoid. I was simply enquiring out of concern for Charlie's welfare as there's been a lot of Prevaricate Pseudologia going about recently.

I get on well with Doctor Richard so I might give him a call and ask if Charlie was tested for it. If not, would you like me to book a follow-up appointment to get it done?

David

**From**: Walter Bowers
**Date**: Tuesday 14 March 2017 11.51am
**To**: David Thorne
**Subject**: Re: ally?

dont have to do that. ill juts antibiotics and if he doesnt get better than I'll take him back. Thanks though.

........................................................................................

**From**: David Thorne
**Date**: Tuesday 14 March 2017 11.54am
**To**: Walter Bowers
**Subject**: Re: Re: ally?

Walter,

It's not a problem at all. Leave it with me.

David

........................................................................................

**From**: Walter Bowers
**Date**: Tuesday 14 March 2017 12.02pm
**To**: David Thorne
**Subject**: Re: Re: Re: ally?

not that its any of your biusness but just so you know i didnt actually go to the vet yesterday. I just said that becasue I was embarrased to say that I hat to go to the doctor for a rash on my groin and Id prefer you didnt say anything to anyone.

**From**: David Thorne
**Date**: Tuesday 14 March 2017 12.09pm
**To**: Walter Bowers
**Subject**: vised story

Walter,

I'm disappointed you felt the need to lie to me but equally impressed by your 'smoke and mirror' deception. You're like the Uri Geller of absenteeism. No, I wont mention your groin rash to anyone. I hope it wasn't anything serious.

David

...................................................................................................

**From**: Walter Bowers
**Date**: Tuesday 14 March 2017 12.21pm
**To**: David Thorne
**Subject**: Re: vised story

no just from riding my bike. a friction rash. Ive had it before.

...................................................................................................

**From**: David Thorne
**Date**: Tuesday 14 March 2017 12.25pm
**To**: Walter Bowers
**Subject**: Re: Re: vised story

Walter,

Did they test for Prevaricate Pseudologia?

David

**From**: Walter Bowers
**Date**: Tuesday 14 March 2017 12.34pm
**To**: David Thorne
**Subject**: Re: Re: Re: vised story

no because Im not a dog. its just a rash. they gave me otment
to put on it.

........................................................................................

**From**: David Thorne
**Date**: Tuesday 14 March 2017 12.40pm
**To**: Walter Bowers
**Subject**: Re: Re: Re: Re: vised story

Walter,

What doctor's office did you go to?

David

........................................................................................

**From**: Walter Bowers
**Date**: Tuesday 14 March 2017 12.47pm
**To**: David Thorne
**Subject**: Re: Re: Re: Re: Re: vised story

none of your busines.

# Kevin's Retorts

Kevin, an account rep at the agency I work for, announced he is retiring next month. He turns sixty-five in January but doesn't look a day over eighty. I told him this and he retorted, "Please, you look like three raccoons wearing a corpse," then dropped a stapler in my coffee. Kevin has a penchant for dropping things in coffee. I've had pens, a mobile phone, a Pantone swatch book, and a hotdog in my cup. The larger items are preferable as I only find the smaller items after I've emptied the cup. Once I found half a box of paperclips in the bottom, which is paramount to attempted murder. While I won't miss having to guard my coffee after he leaves, I will miss Kevin's daily retorts. As such, I decided to document a week's worth:

**New desk photo**
"Is that your family, Kevin?"
"No Mike, it's someone else's family. I just knocked on their front door and asked if I could take a photo."

**The kitchen**
"Last one to use it should have to clean up their mess before the next person. It's just polite."
"Nobody asked about your weekend, Melissa."

### Sandwiches ordered for lunch

"Are you really not going to eat any of them, Kevin?"

"No thank you, mayonnaise monkey."

### Hairdresser appointment

"I'm thinking about getting it cut short."

"Good idea, Jennifer. Let me know if you'd like any beard grooming tips as well."

### 5.20PM

"You still here?"

"No, Walter, I'm a holographic projection. The real Kevin installed magic fucking lasers in the ceiling."

### Cat hair

"You're covered in cat hair, Kevin."

"I'd rather be covered in cat hair than your father's spit, Melissa."

### Archive box

"Can I put this on your desk, Kevin?"

"I doubt it, Ben. With your physique I'm amazed you made it into my office without a lung collapsing."

### Friday evening

"Doing anything on the weekend, Kevin?"

"No, I'll be in suspended animation for forty-eight hours, Mike. I've got a stasis chamber at home that lowers my heart rate to one beat per day. See you in an hour."

# Kevin's Office

As it's Kevin's last week, Ben, Walter and I decided to help him clean out his office. Walter wasn't keen to participate but I threatened to tell Mike about a certain vet appointment if he didn't. Helping Kevin clean out his office entailed staying late a few nights, which is no small feat as I'm not a fan of being at the office at all. Kevin almost caught us once when he returned to the office after forgetting his keys, but we managed to throw his chair massager and coat rack out a window and hide under his desk in time.

**From**: Kevin Eastwood
**Date**: Monday 9 October 2017 10.06am
**To**: All staff
**Subject**: Watering can

The yellow watering can from my office is missing. It's my personal watering can that I brought in from home to water my ficus and I'd appreciate people asking before they use my things. Please return ASAP.

My coffee mug is also nowhere to be found and I know it was on my desk before I left Friday.

Kevin

**From**: Kevin Eastwood
**Date**: Tuesday 10 October 2017 9.18am
**To**: All staff
**Subject**: Missing items

My watering can and coffee mug are still missing. I expect both to be located before the end of the day.

Someone has also taken all of my pens and whiteboard markers and I had stuff in my top drawer and now there's nothing in there except one rubber band.

There's no reason for anyone to enter my office when I'm not here. I will be locking my office door from now on.

Kevin

. . . . . . . . . . . . . . . . .

**From**: Kevin Eastwood
**Date**: Wednesday 11 October 2017 9.07am
**To**: All staff
**Subject**: THIEVES

I expect my office door to be put back on and my family photos returned IMMEDIATELY.

You picked the wrong person to mess with and just crossed the line. I'm filing a formal complaint with Jennifer and when I find out who's doing this, and I will, don't you worry, you're going to be extremely sorry.

Kevin

**From**: Kevin Eastwood
**Date**: Thursday 12 October 2017 9.08pm
**To**: All staff
**Subject**: FUCK YOU ALL

I don't even care who's taking my stuff. Without my desk I can't work so I'm going home. I'm not going to work on the floor. Give yourself a pat on the back. Good job, hope you're happy. Tomorrow's my last day so I expect my personal possessions back before I leave OR ELSE!!!

P.S. If one single leaf on my ficus is missing you are dead.

Kevin

. . . . . . . . . . . . . . . . . .

**From**: Melissa Peters
**Date**: Friday 13 October 2017 9.32am
**To**: All staff
**Subject**: WHERE'S MY STUFF?

I'm sending this from Melissa's computer because I don't have one.

Thank god this is my last day as I've never had to deal with a more juvenile and inept group of halfwits in my life. It's like a day care service for mentally disabled children. You come in, walk around nodding and making stupid faces at each other, and then go home. Last month it took 2 weeks for me to get Inc. added to a brochure. 2 weeks for 3 letters and a dot. Just when I think the art department couldn't possibly get any more fucking useless, you put in extra effort and prove me wrong. Oh, and Walter, I'll be really disappointed if I find out you had anything to do with the theft of my possessions. The rest of you, not so much, you're all a bunch of dishonest, self-serving miscreants. And yes that includes you Mike and Jennifer. I doubt this company will last another year and when it folds, good luck finding work anywhere other than a public bathroom glory hole. You're less use than the talentless inbred monkeys in the art department, wandering around pretending you're doing something and calling meetings to ask what everyone else is doing. Breaking news, people: Nobody is doing anything.

I'm going to wait in the boardroom for 1 HOUR. If all my stuff isn't returned by then, I'm calling the police.

Kevin

. . . . . . . . . . . . . . . . . .

**From**: Kevin Eastwood
**Date**: Friday 13 October 2017 11.22am
**To**: All staff
**Subject**: Drinks

Thank you for the cake. And for loading my car. Sorry about the last email. Looking forward to drinks this afternoon.

Kevin

# Walk it Off, Princess

"What's this?" Holly asked. She held up a large glossy brochure with a cruise ship on the cover. The ship, an icebreaker, was anchored off an ice shelf and tourists were standing on the ice in big puffy jackets with expedition badges on their sleeves, pointing at things and taking photos of penguins. Holly and I were packing to move and the bottom of an old cardboard archive box containing projects I had worked on over the years had given way, spilling its contents onto the basement floor.

"Nothing," I replied.

"Did you design this?"

"Yes, a thousand years ago. Just throw the whole box out."

"Did you get to go to Antarctica?"

"No. We just did the branding and marketing materials."

"When you worked at de Masi jones?"

"No, before that."

Holly flicked through the brochure, "It's really nice. I like how the pictures are matte but certain objects are glossy."

"Spot varnish. It's expensive but it gives a nice effect."

"They should have given you a free trip."

"We were promised a free trip but it never eventuated. Neil Fairhead promised us a lot of things."

"Who's Neil Fairhead?"

"Nobody."

I first met Neil Fairhead, on a scorching summer day, at a local Mexican restaurant called Zapata's. He'd contacted me via email the day before and we'd arranged to meet to discuss 'an exciting opportunity' over lunch. The meeting was set for twelve-thirty; he arrived a little after one. I watched him pull up in a black E-Class Mercedes, climb out, and carefully brush himself down with a lint roller for several minutes before making his way in.

I could describe Neil but it's easier if you just picture a life-sized Howdy Doody bobblehead. I'm not exaggerating; his head was huge and looked like it was twice as close as his body as he headed towards my table. I almost ducked. His neck must have been one solid mass of muscle to support it - but with a non-solid bit through the middle so he could breathe and swallow obviously. If I had a head that size, and neon-red hair like Neil's, I'd wear clothing with muted colours so as not to draw further attention to myself but Neil wore a green suit. Not the dark 'English racing green' sort of green, the 'Kermit the frog green' kind of green.

"I like your suit."
"Thanks. It's Prada."
"Prada make green suits?"
"Yes, it's custom. I have a blue one at home as well."
"Cookie Monster blue or Smurf blue?"
"Somewhere in-between."
"Nice."

He took off his jacket and draped it over a chair. The label was visible and it read Joseph. A. Banks Menswear.

This probably should have been a red flag but I was only twenty-eight at the time, running a small design agency with just four employees, and desperate for new clients.

I'd started the agency three years before by accident really; I was working for a large Australian packaging company called Amcor and had just been promoted to art department manager after the previous manager, Mr Brown, threatened to go home, get his gun, and come back and kill everybody. It was an exciting morning that included Mr Brown being pepper-sprayed by police officers and escorted out in handcuffs. He managed to kick over a water cooler on the way out but he was the only one who got wet. A Channel 9 News crew turned up an hour later but decided the story wasn't as exciting as everyone was making it out to be and left. We got the rest of the day off though, due to the art-department reeking of capsaicin, which was nice as it was a Friday - long weekend and all that.

I was offered Mr Browns position, and a small pay increase, the following Monday morning. By Friday, I understood why Mr Brown had lost the plot. Managing designers is like attempting to produce a Broadway play with the entire cast made up of toddlers; there's tears and tantrums, shit everywhere, and nobody has any idea what they are meant to be doing. The work wasn't hard but there was a lot of it:

Reps emailed the art department details and dimensions of required packaging artwork, a proof was produced and sent back to the rep for approval, then the artwork was sent off to be made into printing plates. Having a team of six designers and around 100 proofs to be completed daily meant a maximum of two hours per design. Designers don't like two-hour deadlines. They also don't like being told that they're "not Neville fucking Brody" and that a cardboard box featuring an arrow and the words 'this way up' doesn't require a forty-five minute group discussion about negative space.

"How's that cucumber box coming along, Adam?"

"You just asked me that."

"That was four hours ago."

"No it wasn't, it was... less than three."

"I asked after you'd been working on it for two hours. I've got that design in the system as a one-hour job. It's a single colour print produce box."

"I'm almost finished. I just have to design the graphic."

"The graphic? What have you been working on?"

"The sides."

The sides say, 'Contents: 40 cucumbers. Handle with care.'"

"And?"

"And I fail to see how that's taken... five hours. How long do you think it will take to do the graphic? Should I check back with you next week?"

"I've got enough on my plate without you being sarcastic."

"And nobody will have cucumbers on their plates unless you get the box done. Seriously, how long is it going to take you to finish it?"

"How long is a piece of string?"

"That's misuse of an idiom, a piece of string can be any length but the time it takes to write the word 'cucumbers' and wack a picture of a cucumber on a box is easily calculable. In this case, one hour."

"I can either do it well or I can do it quickly, which one do you want, David?"

"It's a cucumber box, Adam. I want it done quickly. Nobody gives a fuck if it's done well. The farmer is going to fill it with cucumbers, it's going to be driven to the supermarket, the cucumbers are going to be stacked onto shelves and the box is going to be crushed. You've got ten minutes."

"What? I can't even pick a typeface in ten minutes."

"What typeface did you use for the sides and back?"

"Bauhaus Bold."

"Really?"

"Yes, what's wrong with Bauhaus Bold?"

"Nothing, it's a great font for roller derby posters."

"I'm not changing it."

"No, you're right, we haven't got another three hours. Write 'cucumbers' in Bauhaus Bold, add a picture of a cucumber, and call it done. If anyone asks about it, I'll say you're on medication."

"I'm going to add a sunrise behind the cucumber as well. To give it a 'fresh from the farm' feel."

"No, just whack a cucumber on it and hit print."

"It won't take me long."

"Yes it will. Just whack a cucumber on it, please."

"Right, I'm going to go see Tony."

"What for?"

"To tell him you're micro-managing me and stifling my creativity."

"You'd actually call attention to the fact it's taken you five hours to design a cucumber box to the regional manager? It's a rather odd thing to do but okay, off you go then."

"Fine. But I'm adding a sunrise."

. . . . . . . . . . . . . . . . . . . .

**From**: David Thorne
**Date**: Monday 24 August 1998 9.39am
**To**: Tony Cox
**Subject**: Resignation

Morning Tony,

Firstly, thank you for the opportunities you have provided me here at Amcor. I've gained an in-depth knowledge of the flexographic printing industry over the last two years and taking over the position of Art Department Manager last month has proved an interesting and challenging experience.

However, as a graphic designer, managing other graphic designers is not the career path I envisioned and I think it may be time for me to move on. Please let me know what processes and paperwork need to be completed.

Regards, David

**From**: Tony Cox
**Date**: Monday 24 August 1998 10.21am
**To**: David Thorne
**Subject**: Re: Resignation

David,

What the fuck? Why are you quitting? The art dept. is running like clockwork. The backlog has been cleared and productivity is up 30%. Have you been offered another job?

Tony

....................................................................................................

**From**: David Thorne
**Date**: Monday 24 August 1998 10.46am
**To**: Tony Cox
**Subject**: Re: Re: Resignation

Tony,

The only clockwork the art department could be likened to would be that off a $5 knock-off Rolex from Indonesia. One that accidently got worn while swimming.

My position wasn't replaced when I took Andrew's role and Adam quit last week citing 'creative differences'. Hayley sits at her desk sobbing most days and Christine manages to get through about a proof a week as she has no idea how to use a computer. I've tried to show her but she's 72 and doesn't give a fuck. Apparently she used to be the tea lady here in the 60s and just sat down one day.

Frank and Yola are the only ones getting proofs out and what they don't complete, I've been taking home with me and doing in the evening.

I realise my decision creates a difficult situation but I will do whatever I can to help with the transition over the next few weeks.

And no, I haven't been offered another job. I'm not sure what I'm going to do actually. I have a decent setup at home though so I might give freelance a go until I find another design position.

Regards, David

....................

Tony outsourced work to me. It started with ten or eleven proofs a day - just to take the load off the art-department - then a few more when Christine died. She had diseased gums and the infection made its way to her heart - which stopped while she was on the phone arguing with a rep about why a typeface change to a proof was taking two weeks. Frank told me that her last words were, "I'm not a fucking robot."

Hayley left the art department next, apparently God told her to build huts on an island somewhere in the Pacific Ocean. I hadn't even realised she was religious and I'm pretty sure I used the term, "Jesus fucking Christ, Hayley, what is it now?"

at least five times a day when I'd been there. She wasn't replaced and the amount of proofs sent to me increased.

....................

From: Frank Goodwin
Date: Wednesday 21 October 1998 11.02am
To: David Thorne
Subject: fuck this place

Hey.

Just so you know, I'm quitting as well so you're probably going to get a lot more proofs in two weeks. Did Yola tell you they moved us into the cafeteria? This is bullshit. They put those moveable walls up but we can still hear people eating on the other side and they look through the cracks. Im using one of the plastic tables as a desk. How is this even remotely acceptable?

Also, the lady at the cafeteria says you still owe her $6.50 for a kitchener bun and coke. I'm not paying it for you.

Frank

....................

Frank came to work with me and we easily dealt with the seventy or so proofs per day between us. Yola found out and was pissed so she became my second employee.

Amcor shut down the art department completely. There wasn't much point having one when the three of us managed 100% of the work load. Frank and Yola were hard workers; we had gotten along well at Amcor and the only thing that had changed was the environment. It was a better environment, a more relaxed work space where people came and went as they pleased based on the workload for the day. Without a clock-in clock-out mentality, we were a lot more efficient - sometimes we'd have that day's proofs completed by mid afternoon and could take the rest of the day off but just as often we'd work until past midnight. Neither Frank or Yola complained when we had late nights as they were making almost double what they'd made at Amcor. Frank bought his first new car, Yola purchased an apartment. We all did alright out of it; I was saving to buy a house and had around two-hundred grand in my personal account after three years. I'd registered as a business by then, moved from the home office into a real office with a sign on the door and employed a third person - a young Chinese woman named Huang - to do payroll and accounts. I say 'young' but none of us could work out her age - Asian women look 16 until they hit 50, at which point they immediately jump to 105. Whenever anyone asked Huang her age, she'd reply, "How old you think I am?" and then when you took a polite guess, she'd state, "You stupid" which never answered the question. She probably thought she was being all 'mystery of the Orient' or something. We'd advertised the position and received a few written applications but Huang had just showed up at the office with an abacus.

"You test me."

"That won't be necessary, this is just an informal cha..."

"You test me."

"Right, okay, what's 97 times 18?"

...cht, cht, cht...

"1,746."

"Is she correct, Frank?"

"I don't know, I don't do math."

"I correct every time. You gave me test for children. Give me harder test."

"Well, there's not really much point as we don't know if you're getting them right."

"I right every time. Give me harder test."

"Fine, what's 95,000,000 divided by 267,303?"

"That stupid. You no have 95,000,000 dollars. I start today."

"We actually have a few people to see but..."

"Nobody else want to work here. It stink. You smoke in office?"

"Er, Frank and I do sometimes but..."

"I start today."

"We haven't even discussed pay."

"500 dollars a week. Cash."

"Frank, how much does that work out to per year?"

"That's 500 times 52 so... wait, is there 52 weeks in a year or is that how many cards are in a pack?"

"Yola, how much does that work out to per year?"

"It's 2K per month so that's 24K... which is actually very reasonable."

"That can't be right. There's more than four weeks in a

month. Except February. The other months have four weeks plus a couple of days. Maybe three. What's 12 months divided by 52 weeks?"

"What?"

"See? This is why we need someone to do our accounts."

"I start today. Tomorrow I bring pohpia."

"Who's that?"

"No who. Spring rolls."

"Okay."

Most men have a thing for Asian women (not Asian porn though, nobody wants to hear that dreadful "eeh-eeh-eeh" noise all the way through the video), but Huang wasn't the type of Asian anyone has anything for; she was short and round and her teeth looked like fat porcupine quills. She also turned out to be quite mean - yelling and calling us stupid - but she was good at her job and had imported all of our accounts into software that was written in Mandarin within the first week so there wasn't much we could do about it even if we wanted to.

Amcor grew, which meant our workload grew. I took on a fourth employee, Justin, to cope. Justin was Yola's younger brother and everyone suspected he might have slight Down syndrome. I'm not sure if you can have slight Down syndrome, or if it's a black and white thing where you either have it or you don't, but I've seen people with Down syndrome bagging groceries in supermarkets and people with Down syndrome that can't do much of anything except smile and eat ice cream. The ones with ice creams usually have really thick glasses. There's obviously a scale of capability with people who *don't* have Down syndrome - some are intelligent, educated and articulate functioning members of society, some are in the middle, and some voted for Trump - so perhaps Justin was just at the intelligent, educated and articulate end of the Down syndrome scale which made it hard to tell. If *I'd* been born with Down syndrome I'd be the kind that gets shown on the news playing a game of junior baseball for a local team and one of the kids would say, "We don't even think of him as different, he's just a member of the team." Then they'd show me hitting a ball thrown softly underarm and everyone would cheer as I ran the wrong way and shit myself. At the end of the news segment, I'd be lifted onto the shoulders of my teammates, beaming and pumping the air with a fist, possibly while holding an ice cream, and the reporter would say something about the power of friendship. Coincidentally, it's also difficult to tell the age of people with Down syndrome; they all look like 50-year-old men, even the women. I think part of the problem is that they don't use hair product.

Regardless, Justin's scale of capability in no way affected his ability to put together proofs. Quite the opposite in fact; Justin was like a machine, averaging five proofs an hour and pausing only to smile and wave when someone walked past his desk. With his first pay, he purchased 75 boxes of white Christmas lights and strung them from the office ceiling.

"What the fuck is this?"

"Christmas lights."

"It's June."

"I like them."

"It's like the patio of a Mexican cantina in here. All we need is a Mariachi band and an old man trying to convince us to buy cellophane wrapped roses for our señoritas. Our power bill is going to triple."

"Do you want me to take them down?"

"No, I suppose not. I kind of like them, too."

"Can I put up more?"

"No."

Frank wore sunglasses for two days to prove a point so we ended up buying dimmers. A few months later one of the dimmers caught fire - possibly from having enough current running through it to kick-start a fusion reactor - but Huang put it out with a large ceramic pot of water-lily and shiitake mushroom soup.

Apart from the odd fire and extreme power bills, we did actually have an art department that 'ran like clockwork'. Maybe not Swiss-made clockwork but a decent Japanese movement. There were the usual petty arguments of course, Yola put Frank in a headlock until he passed out once and Huang quit about three-hundred times... but not once *in three years* had we failed to complete our proof quota for the day. Sure we only had one client, which meant all our eggs were in one basket, but it was a pretty big basket...

**From**: Jason Pritchett
**Date**: Tuesday 15 May 2001 12.37pm
**To**: David Thorne
**Subject**: Proof delivery

Dear Mr. Thorne,

My name is Jason Pritchett. I took over Tony Cox's position as regional manager in March.

Part of my role at Amcor is to reduce production costs and one of the areas we have been looking at is the outsourcing of design. Our New Zealand branch began trialing a Malaysian agency for all electronic proof delivery in February and have been pleased with both the results and a 70% cost savings.

In an effort to coordinate all outsourced work through our new production department in Melbourne, Amcor will be contracting all production of proofs to the Malaysian agency exclusively. This is effective immediately. Please complete any outstanding Amcor work you may have and return within the next 7 days. Please also note than any electronic files pertaining to Amcor remain the property of such and should also be returned.

We thank you for the work you have provided Amcor over the last few years and wish you and your agency all the best.

Should you have any future packaging requirements, please do not hesitate to contact us.

Yours, Jason Pritchett

**From**: David Thorne
**Date**: Tuesday 15 May 2001 12.56pm
**To**: Jason Pritchett
**Subject**: Re: Proof delivery

Dear Jason,

I received your email. Congratulations on the promotion to regional manager. And on managing to save Amcor seventy-percent on the cost of proof design and delivery.

I obviously can't compete with Malaysian pricing - not without cutting my employees wages to a bowl of rice per day and instigating beatings - but a little more notice would have been appreciated.

I'm not sure what to tell my four staff members so I might just pile them into a van, drive out into the forest, and leave them there to fend for themselves.

Regards, David

...........................................................................................................

**From**: Jason Pritchett
**Date**: Tuesday 15 May 2001 2.44pm
**To**: David Thorne
**Subject**: Re: Re: Proof delivery

We're not under any legal obligation to give you any notice. Amcor is a global company and our suppliers need to compete on a global level. All the best.

Jason

**From**: David Thorne
**Date**: Tuesday 15 May 2001 3.37pm
**To**: Jason Pritchett
**Subject**: Re: Re: Re: Proof delivery

Jason,

Yes, I understand Amcor is a global company. We did the brochures.

Would you be willing to extend the cutoff of proof delivery to us for three months? This may allow me time to prepare the business for the loss of our single client and seek alternative commissions.

I'd be willing to drop our fees by 30% for this period as a compromise. I have four people working for me, people with mortgages and car payments to make, and this puts me in a very difficult position.

Regards, David

..................................................................................................

**From**: Jason Pritchett
**Date**: Tuesday 15 May 2001 4.28pm
**To**: David Thorne
**Subject**: Re: Re: Re: Re: Proof delivery

I'm unable to change procedures that have already been implemented. I do however wish you all the best in your future endeavors. There is no need to reply to this email.

Jason

We were okay for a few months; I did a lot of legwork and made a lot of calls. We were commissioned by a food manufacturer named Bellis to do their packaging design for a line of fruit bars, and label designs for a large winery in the Barossa Valley named Yaldara, but the work wasn't consistent and the money began to run out. A few fruit bar and wine label designs might have been enough to keep me afloat if I'd been working freelance, but with four employees wages and rent to cover, it wasn't even close. I stopped paying myself and unplugged Justin's lights. The others took pay cuts while we "worked through a rough patch", but they had no idea how rough it was, I was supplementing their wages out of my personal savings at that point. I lost a lot of sleep, and weight. I lied a lot.

And then Neil Fairhead contacted me.

A man named Andrew Tobin gave Neil my contact details. Andrew ran a small Adelaide based publishing company called National Direct that I'd done a bit of 'quick & dirty' work for over the years. He once gave me two weeks to design a book titled *Learn To Play Tennis With Patrick Rafter* which seems like a reasonable time-frame except I had to take the photos, design the layout, *and* write the entire thing. Pages 20 through 37 just contain mathematical formula for calculating wind speed that I copied from a meteorological website and most of the close-up photos of Patrick Rafter's hand holding a tennis racket are actually just me holding a broom.

For those unfamiliar with Patrick Rafter, he's an Australian tennis player who did alright in the 90s. He was a model and spokesperson for Hayne's underwear for a while after that but now he's too old and fat. When I met with him to take the instructional photographs, he was a bit of a dick and told me, "I really don't have time for this shit, I don't even know why I agreed to do it - you've got five minutes." Hence the broom photos and the bit in his bio about collecting pinecones and having a pet sheep named Sheryl that shares his bed.

....................

**From**: Neil Fairhead
**Date**: Thursday 9 August 2001 2.01pm
**To**: David Thorne
**Subject**: Branding work

Hello David,

I hope you don't mind me contacting you out of the blue, Andrew Tobin gave me your email address.

I'm the director of S.A.S.C and I was wondering if we could meet to discuss a project we're working on. We require a full suite of advertising material, brochures, logo and stationery as we are about to go to market with a new tourism venture.

Is this something you'd be interested in?

Neil Fairhead, Director
Southern Australia Shipping Company

**From**: David Thorne
**Date**: Thursday 9 August 2001 2.37pm
**To**: Neil Fairhead
**Subject**: Re: Branding work

Hello Neil,

Thank you for your email. I would certainly be happy to meet and discuss your design requirements. We don't have a shipping company in our portfolio and it sounds like an interesting project.

Would 12.30pm tomorrow at your office suit?

Regards, David

................................................................................

**From**: Neil Fairhead
**Date**: Thursday 9 August 2001 3.09pm
**To**: David Thorne
**Subject**: Re: Re: Branding work

David,

12.30 is great but our offices are being painted at the moment. Let's meet for lunch instead at Zapatas in North Adelaide.

I look forward to meeting you then.

Neil Fairhead, Director
Southern Australia Shipping Company

I paid for lunch. With the volume of work we'd discussed, it seemed the right thing to do. It had also somehow seemed more like a pitch from Neil for me to take on his project than me pitching to take it on, but I put that down to his excitement for the project. It *was* an exciting project, the scope of which included the branding and livery of their new ship, sales brochures, website, stationery... enough work to keep the agency busy for a few months. Nobody had to fend for themselves in a forest just yet.

The Southern Australian Shipping Company... actually, I'm just going to refer to it as SASC from here on as typing out the whole name is already annoying. Sometimes I use made up keywords instead of long names and just do a global word replace at the end but in the first edition of my last book, I forgot to do the change afterwards and the company name Philip Morris International was referred to as 'puffmop' throughout.

SASC, with financing from dozens of National and International investors, had purchased a retired Russian icebreaker for US$35 million. At the time of our meeting, the ship was on route from Russian waters to South Australia with an expected arrival time of eight weeks. It was then going to be refitted for tourism purposes and provide expedition cruises from South Australia to Antarctica. The cruises included trips out onto the ice-shelf to visit Emperor penguin colonies and had the backing of the Australian Geographic Society.

**From**: David Thorne
**Date**: Monday 13 August 2001 10.18am
**To**: Neil Fairhead
**Subject**: Proposal

Hello Neil,

Thank you for meeting with me on Friday. My team is excited by the project and keen to get started.

As requested, please find attached our proposal for the branding work required. I've broken it down into the three stages discussed.

Feel free to call if you have any questions. Once we have approval and the 25% deposit, we can get started on stage one immediately.

Regards, David

## Proposal

**Client**: Southern Australian Shipping Company
**Date**: August 13 2001
**Scope**: Branding, livery, stationery, promotional materials, sales brochures, website etc.

*Stage 1*. Branding

Name development ............................................... $1500.00
Logo creation (includes corporate style guide)........ $2800.00
Stationery suite ..................................................... $1300.00
Sub total: $5600.00

*Stage 2.* Marketing materials

Ship livery mockup (for brochure photos etc)..........$500.00
Brochure design & layout (24 page, full colour) .... $3700.00
Corporate folder ...................................................... $400.00
Itinerary brochures (design & layout @$380 x 4)... $1520.00
Domain name registration and transfer ................... $125.00
Hosting setup and fees ............................................ $238.00
Website design, build and implementation ........... $3600.00
Promotional items (caps, pens, etc.)........................ $260.00

Sub total: $10,343.00

*Stage 3.* Application

Ship livery design (application to scale) ................. $2800.00
Shuttle boat livery design (application to scale)........ $900.00
Uniform design ....................................................... $600.00
Signage ............................................................... $2360.00
On-board branding (estimated) ........................... $4000.00

Sub total: $10,660.00

Combined total (stages 1,2 and 3) .................... $26,603.00
GST................................................................... $2660.30

**Total amount:** $29,263.30

Stage 1 completion date: August 31 2001
Stage 2 completion date: October 12 2001
Stage 3 completion date (estimated): Early November*

* Based on ship arrival date.

**From**: Neil Fairhead
**Date**: Monday 13 August 2001 11.06am
**To**: David Thorne
**Subject**: Re: Proposal

David,

Excellent. Thank you for sending that through. I give approval to go ahead with all stages.

The only problem I see is that we need the stationery, brochure, corporate folder and itinerary brochures before the next investor meeting on September 7th. The success of that meeting depends on having these sales materials. I should have mentioned this during lunch.

Are you able to meet this deadline?

Neil Fairhead, Director
Southern Australia Shipping Company

...............................................................................................................

**From**: David Thorne
**Date**: Monday 13 August 2001 11.28am
**To**: Neil Fairhead
**Subject**: Re: Re: Proposal

Hello Neil,

September 7 is 25 days away. We need to complete the branding before we can even look at marketing materials and printers usually require 7 days lead time - even for short runs.

To have the stationery, corporate folder and brochures back from the printers in time for your investor meeting, we'd need to send finished artwork off no later than the end of this month.

That's 17 days from now.

I'd have to chain my employees in and hook them up to drips of methamphetamine - and even then I'm not sure it's possible - but I'll discuss the timeframe with them and get back to you today.

Regards, David

. . . . . . . . . . . . . . . . . . .

We agreed to the timeframe of course, we didn't have much choice. There was a bit of panic when I told everyone - Frank did a weird thing like the robot dance, but really quickly, then threw up in the bathroom, Yola rocked back and forth on her chair while staring at the ceiling for ten minutes, and Huang yelled at me. I think Justin was playing Dance Dance Revolution in the 'Fun Room' at the time.

Several months earlier, after Frank had gone on and on about how Google has pool tables and fun stuff for their employees to use, I put a Playstation and dance mat in the stationery cupboard and a sign on the door that read, *Fun Room. For employee use.* It was a walk-in stationery cupboard with almost enough room to lay the mat out completely flat, and it's good to be really close to the screen, so Frank's disdain was completely unwarranted. Surprisingly, the person who used the Fun Room the most was Huang. We'd all crowd in the doorway, cheering her on to another perfect score as her legs blurred and arms thrashed to *Boom Boom Dollar* by King Kong and D. Jungle Girls. Sometimes she'd yell at us and close the door but she'd have to open it again a short time later as the Fun Room had no ventilation. I tried it once but I was born without rhythm and apparently looked like I was running through mud while carrying buckets.

"Why are you lifting your knees so high?"

"To press the pad things."

"You don't need to stomp, just slide."

"I can't, my socks have little rubber dots on the bottom to give them grip."

"You look like you're climbing a fence."

"No, he looks more like he's playing a giant Whack-A-Mole game with his whole body. Or running through mud while carrying buckets."

"Right, fuck this then. Someone else have a turn."

"The song hasn't finished yet. Play it through."

"No, I hate it."

"Weak."

"Fuck you, Frank. I haven't seen you play once."

"That's because I'm claustrophobic."

We tackled the naming first, usually this would consist of two or three days of research then a day of brainstorming but we simply didn't have that luxury.

"Right, we have an hour to come up with a name. Something that screams, 'Let's visit Antarctica and look at penguins'. Shout out names and I'll make a list on the white board."

"What about *Penguin*."

"Yes, excellent Yola, 'all aboard the *Penguin*,' when people ask, 'Oh, you went to Antarctica?', travellers can answer, 'Yes, we took the *Penguin*'... actually that's not as bad as it first seemed, I apologise for the sarcasm, I'll write it down. Anybody else? Yes, Justin? You don't have to raise your hand, just shout names out."

"*Ice Explorer*."

"Right. I'll write it down but..."

"Or *Penguin Explorer*."

"Okay, that's a bit suggestive but I'll add it... yes Frank?"

"How about *Hubert*?"

"Why would we name the ship after a cartoon bear?"

"That's Rupert. Hubert Wilkins was a famous South Australian explorer."

"Did he explore Antarctica?"

"He might have."

"We're not calling the ship *Hubert*. I'm not even going to write it down."

"You wrote down *Penguin Explorer*."

"Fine. I'll add it. Anyone else? Yes, Huang?"

"You need me here? I play Dance Dance Revolution."

"That's fine, just keep the volume down. Right, we have *Penguin*, *Ice Explorer*, *Penguin Explorer* and *Hubert* so obviously this isn't working. Let's just make a list of things you'd see in Antarctica... yes, Yola?"

"Penguins."

"Alright, we'll start with that..."

"...and ice."

"Good, keep them coming."

"Polar bears."

"There's no polar bears in Antarctica, Frank."

"Who says?"

"It's just a fact. There's only seals and penguins.

"Seals then."

"Okay. Yes, Justin?"

"Big puffy jackets."

"...right."

"...and scarves."

"Really, Justin?"

"To keep your face warm."

"Fine, I'll add big puffy jackets and scarves to the list. And beanies, gloves and thick socks to save time..."

"...and stars. Ships used to navigate by the stars and you'd be able to see the constellations really clearly in Antarctica without any light pollution from the cities."

"What the fuck? That's not bad, Justin. Have you been holding out on us?"

"...especially the Southern Cross."

"Right, everyone's fired apart from Justin. We're calling the ship *The Southern Australis* and using the Southern Cross as the logo. Done and dusted... yes, Yola?"

"I think the logo should have a penguin in it as well."

"Fine. Throw together a logo of a penguin looking up at the Southern Cross and I'll get it to Neil for approval."

**From**: David Thorne
**Date**: Wednesday 15 August 2001 3.12am
**To**: Neil Fairhead
**Subject**: Naming and logo development

Morning Neil,

Unless you're especially fond of the name *Hubert*, we're leaning towards *The Southern Australis* as the name of the ship. It's sophisticated, distinctly South Australian, and reminiscent of a time when expedition ships navigated by the stars. We've registered the .com and .com.au - these can be allowed to expire if we go with an alternative name.

Rough logo concept attached. We've used a crisp blue (PMS 299) to represent water & ice, and yellow (PMS 121) for the secondary text and subtle gradient on the Emperor penguin's chest. It also works well in single colour and reversed.

Let me know your thoughts and any changes required. In order to proceed with the promotional materials and have them completed before the 31st, we need to lock this stage down as soon as possible.

Regards, David

From: Neil Fairhead
Date: Wednesday 15 August 2001 9.17am
To: David Thorne
Subject: Re: Naming and logo development

David,

It's perfect. I love the name and the logo. I think I like the one in the circle better but they are both great. Well done. Let's run with it.

I can see by the time you sent that email that you were up late working and I appreciate your team's efforts.

I spoke to the other directors and we've all agreed to give you and your staff complimentary cabins on the ship's first cruise to Antarctica in February. The first trip will be a test run but this means you and about 10 other guests will have the whole ship to yourselves. All you'd have to do is give feedback about the trip to iron out any kinks so that we can make sure the first commercial voyage is perfect.

Looking forward to seeing the brochure and other promotional materials. I'll send through copy and photos for the brochures by Friday.

How hard would it be to get business cards done by next Thursday? I only need ones with my name and details at this stage. If it's too much bother I can wait until everything is printed.

Neil Fairhead, Director
Southern Australia Shipping Company

**From**: David Thorne
**Date**: Wednesday 15 August 2001 10.12am
**To**: Neil Fairhead
**Subject**: Re: Re: Naming and logo development

Hello Neil,

I'm glad you're happy with the direction - the logo is a bit rough but we'll tweak it over the next few days. The penguin was meant to be looking up and it's all looking a little too Star Trek. We'd usually present a completed logo showing application but time didn't permit.

The enclosed logo, in the circle, is just a quick example of application. The open identity will be used for the majority of corporate application and the enclosed 'expedition' version for commercial application, embroidered patches, caps, etc.

I'll have Frank create and send you business card artwork this afternoon. We can have these digitally printed and to you by next week if you only need a small batch. Huang is also sending you a revised invoice for the 25% deposit today. It combines stage 1 and 2 components that we are working on. It's a 14 day invoice but as we've already started the project, having it processed sooner would be appreciated.

Also, thank you very much for the complimentary cabin offer. I'm sure everyone here will be excited by the prospect. Will we need to bring our own big puffy jackets or will these will be supplied?

Regards, David

I told Yola that Neil hated the logo and wanted a ship with dolphins jumping out of the water beside it. It was meant to be a quick joke but after she tore an AC temperature control unit off the wall, I had her work on the logo for a few hours.

"That's coming along well. I think the dolphin should be a lot larger though."

"Larger? It's already twice the size of the ship."

"Then make the ship larger as well."

"What?"

"Oh, and Neil hates the typeface. Try Baskerville Bold or maybe Bauhaus in... are you crying?"

"I wish I was dead. I can't stand it anymore."

"Right, well I feel terrible now. I was joking about the penguin logo, Neil approved it."

"What?"

"Yes, it was just a joke. He loved it. Good job."

"I've been working on this for two hours. You made me watch a video of dolphins jumping out of waves."

"You ripped the AC unit out of the wall."

"Yes, because you told me he wanted a fucking dolphin logo."

"Fine, let's just agree that we're both at fault."

"No, I quit."

"Don't be like that, Yola. What if I organise tickets for all of us on the *Southern Australis* for its first cruise to Antarctica? Would that make it up to you?"

"Really?"

"Consider it done. Also, Frank's not back from lunch yet so I'm going to need you to design a business card."

The next two weeks were a blur of late nights and grumpy mornings. Floors were strewn with printouts and desks piled with empty pizza boxes, styrofoam coffee cup towers, and overflowing ashtrays. Yola took up smoking on day four of the sales brochure design and by the end of the fortnight, was on four packs a day.* Frank and I had been the only smokers before this so it was quite convenient for us as it meant we didn't have to go outside to smoke anymore. At times, the smoke in the office was so thick we wouldn't have been able to find the exit if we'd wanted to. We hung several air-fresheners shaped like pine trees around Huang's desk but she still complained. Justin had a Ventalin inhaler so he was fine. We let him crack a window near his desk whenever he had an asthma attack - only for a bit though because it was pretty warm outside and the AC temperature control unit was broken. Frank tried to reconnect it but when he reached into the hole in the wall, there must have been loose wires because he received a decent shock. I gave him a stick of butter to rub into his third-degree burns, as that's the recommended thing to do, but there wasn't much that could

---

* Say what you will about smokers, we don't care, a smoker is far more productive if allowed to chain-smoke at their desk. Otherwise, they're just killing time until they feel it's been long enough to go outside and have a cigarette without non-smoking coworkers giving them 'the look' or stating, "You're going outside again?" Yes I'm going outside again, bitch, this is what you and your fellow non-smoking cult members have forced me to become; I could have had six weeks work done in the last four hours but instead I've ordered a pair of pants on Amazon and read a Wikipedia article about bamboo.

be done in-house for his tongue - he was poking it out between his teeth when he received the shock and bit clean through the tip. It wasn't a large chunk, only about the size of a baby slug, but I still agreed to drive him to the hospital. His screaming was distracting everyone from their work anyway. I'd first suggested dipping his tongue - the bit he still had, not the bit now in his hand - in melted candle wax to seal the end, but Frank insisted he wanted the tip stitched back on. Unfortunately, while climbing out of my car at the hospital, Frank dropped the bit of tongue down the side of his car seat. We looked for it for a about ten minutes before giving up and heading inside - I thought I'd found it at one point and held it up to Frank excitedly but it turned out to be a wad of chewing gum. I was a bit annoyed about this as Huang was the only person in the office who chewed gum and she'd borrowed my car for errands the previous week while her scooter was in the shop.

"It just shows a lack of respect for other people's property."

"Nnnnnn n nnn nnnn nnnaaa."

"The nurse said the doctor will see you shortly, just be patient. There's a vending machine over there, do want a packet of crisps while we wait?"

"N n nneh nnnth?"

"Oh, right. I wouldn't mind some though, do you have any change on you? I found some under the car seat but I didn't think to bring it in. No? Anyway, my point is, that if someone's nice enough to loan you their car, there's rules you have to abide by. Rule number one is that you don't just spit your disgusting wad of chewed gum down the side of the seat. It shouldn't even have to be a rule, it should just be obvious, but it's people like Huang who make these rules necessary. Rule number two is that you return the vehicle with a full tank, not potting mix on the back seat. How hard is it to put down a towel or something? There's a third rule but I can't remember what that is."

"Nnnnn naaa nhhhhnn?"

"Yes, it's bleeding a lot. Just hold the kitchen sponge against it tighter. Which hurts worse, the arm or the tongue?"

"Nnth."

"Well there's nothing we can do about your tongue until the doctor sees you but I could walk down to the cafeteria and see if they have any of those single-serve butter sachets. How many do you reckon you'd need? Ten?"

"Nn. Nh nahh nks eh nhh."

"Nonsense, how can the butter make it worse? Never mind, here's the doctor now. Should I wait for you or can you make your own way back?"

"Nnn nn nthn?"

"I'm kidding. I'll wait. Probably in the car though as sick people have touched everything in here."

I found the tip of Frank's tongue while I was waiting; it was wedged between the seat and backrest and hadn't gone down the side at all. I opened the passenger door and flicked it out with a pen. After an hour or so I went to Burger King and when I got back, Frank was waiting by the hospital entrance in a wheelchair, which was a little dramatic. There was nothing wrong with his legs and the burns on his arm hadn't been as bad as they seemed. They'd bandaged it though, and his tongue.

"It looks like a giant maggot is poking out of your mouth. Especially when you move it like that."

"Nn nn nhh?"

"Yes, in a minute, just let me finish my Whopper. Good job on the brochure by the way. It turned out well. Neil signed off on it straight away so it's ready for pre-press."

"Hnn nnh n nnhhn?"

"Everything's signed off. Yola's sending all the other artwork to the printers today and if we get the brochure off tomorrow, it means we met deadline. We should all go out tonight and celebrate."

"Nh nh nhn."

"Oh, right. Maybe tomorrow night then if you're up to it. It'll be my shout for all the hard work everyone's done. Yola slept at her desk the last three nights and I know you've been working till three or four in the morning since the project began. Everyone stepped up; Justin is a Photoshop Jedi and Huang must have made us a thousand pots of coffee."

"Nhn n nhh eh nhh?"

"No, not yet. They can only approve invoices during monthly director meetings. I agreed to cover the 17K printing costs and add on 10%. Do you want these fries?"

"Nh hhnn nhh."

"Oh, right. I think your tongue is still bleeding a bit. It looks like a giant maggot wearing lipstick now."

**From:** David Thorne
**Date:** Friday 31 August 2001 2.40pm
**To:** Neil Fairhead
**Subject:** Press checks

Morning Neil,

Just letting you know all artwork has been sent to the printers. I spoke to Joseph at Finsbury and they are adding a spot varnish as requested. It's an extra plate but worth it. They'll have the brochure on press Monday and I will be at the press check. The corporate folder, stationery and itineraries are on press Tuesday. They've guaranteed delivery by Thursday so that works out perfectly.

Also, have you had a chance to look at the 25% deposit invoice Huang sent you a few weeks ago?

Regards, David

...............................................................................................

**From:** Neil Fairhead
**Date:** Friday 31 August 2001 3.19pm
**To:** David Thorne
**Subject:** Re: Press checks

David,

Looking forward to seeing the finished product. That invoice was approved during our director meeting yesterday and was sent to our accounts department so you should receive a cheque within 14 days. I made a note that it's a priority.

I also wanted to discuss an exciting opportunity that I think you might be interested in. Would you be able to meet me for lunch on Wednesday to discuss?

Does 12.30 at Zapata's work for you?

Neil Fairhead, Director
Southern Australia Shipping Company

..................................................................................

**From**: David Thorne
**Date**: Friday 31 August 2001 4.07pm
**To**: Neil Fairhead
**Subject**: Re: Re: Press checks

Neil,

Sounds good, I'll see you Wednesday. Have a good weekend.

Regards, David

...................

Frank *was* up for celebrating that night. As were Yola and Justin. Hoang was invited but she never went anywhere with us. As she put it, "People see me with you, they think I stupid too." which is obviously the Mystic East version of being judged by the company you keep. We went to a hotel called *The Grace Emily* as it was one of the few places in Adelaide that smoking hadn't been banned. It was sticky, dirty and smelly but so were the people who went there which meant not having to dress up. Occasionally you'd see someone well dressed, but only as they walked in, looked around in horror, and walked out again shuddering. Art students liked the place as nobody judged them when they counted out change to pay for their pint and rolled their own cigarettes. Apart from me of course, I was a bit judgy; I once saw an art student wax their armpits at the bar, which is crossing the social etiquette line as far as I'm concerned. Someone stuck one of the used hairy blobs of wax on a window and it remained there for so many years it became a landmark on busy nights.

"Where's Yola?"

"She's talking to a fat guy in skinny jeans. Two tables to the left of the hairy wax blob."

"Oh yeah. Where's Frank?"

"He's being told off by a member of the Lesbian Knitting Club for spilling beer in her yarn basket. Underneath the poster of the horse sucking off a cowboy."*

Frank wasn't supposed to have alcohol while on Oxycodone but there was no way he was missing out if I was paying. Drinking beer through a straw may sound awkward but he was actually able to down a pint in less than two seconds.

---

* *The poster hadn't originally been of a horse sucking off a cowboy. It was originally an advertisement for Stetson hats – of a cowboy giving his horse a drink from his hat – but someone had changed the text 'The last drop from his Stetson' to 'The last drop from his cock' and drawn a penis on the cowboy, ejaculating into the horse's mouth.*

When he eventually passed out in the bathroom, someone drew a little smiley face on his tongue bandage with a Sharpie.

A guy named Wilson drew on my face with a permanent marker while I was passed out drunk on a couch once. He also shaved off my eyebrows but was kind enough to draw on a new set. I get that it's hilarious for the artist, but the unwilling canvas has enough on their plate to deal with the next morning without having to go to work with Spock eyebrows and the words, "Beam me up, Scotty" written on their cheek. Also, if you are going to do to this to someone, don't get drunk and pass out at a party a week later when the victim is present. It took over an hour to shave Wilson's head and super glue on a swimming cap - then another hour to super glue his hair back on top of that - but quality work takes time. I wasn't there when he woke up the next morning but apparently he didn't notice anything different - even after using the bathroom - until his scalp began to itch. Then several pieces of furniture were smashed and the police called to remove him from the premises. I saw him at a supermarket a few weeks later, he was wearing a baseball cap but you could still see bits of rubber stuck to the back of his neck. I ducked behind a display of pasta sauce because it's always awkward bumping into people you know at the supermarket. Especially if you exchange formalities and then have to pass them again several times in different aisles. Usually I'll just abandon my cart and go home after the first round. Sometimes I wear a disguise though.

"Is Frank okay?"

"He's fine, Yola. I offered to call him a taxi but he said he just wants to have a quick rest and then he'll be out for another beer. Who was the fat guy in skinny jeans you were talking to earlier? The one with the Carol Brady haircut."

"Thomas de Masi. I know his brother, Nik. He was showing me news clippings about himself."

"He carries around news clippings about himself to show people? Why are you still here and not in his bed?"

"I know, right?"

"What were the news clippings about? Court rulings on the distance he has to stay away from schools?"

"He runs a small agency down the street called de Masi jones. They did the public transport livery design."

"Nice. If you dated him, you might get a travel discount on bus rides during non-peak hours."

"His brother Nik had an art exhibition a few months back. He's actually a very talented artist."

"Speaking of which, someone's drawn a smiley face on Frank's tongue bandage - it looks hilarious. I wish my phone had a camera. Have you seen those, Justin? Camera phones?"

"No."

"I read about them in *Wired*, they're coming out next year apparently. You can take a photo with your phone and send it to anyone. I bet by the year 2010 we'll all have phones that have the Internet."

"Why would anyone want to look at photos or the Internet on a tiny phone screen?"

"By 2010 there won't be a screen, you'll wear the phone on

your wrist, like a bracelet, and a microchip in your eye will display the information as if it's floating a few feet from your face - you'll control it by hand and head movements, or possibly by thought. Ten years is a long time technology-wise, have you seen that graph thing with the curve?"

"No."

"It's a graph that shows technology increases over the last two-thousand years. We'd all be living on space stations and have personal nano-dust by now if it wasn't for religion."

"What's nano-dust?"

"Millions of nanomites, tiny robots the size of dust, that float around you. You can hardly see them but they're programmed so that if you think of a chair, they form together to make a chair. Say you're outside and it starts to rain, pop, you've got an umbrella."

"Like magic?"

"No, like science. Any sufficiently advanced technology is indistinguishable from magic though, it's one of Clarke's three laws."

"Clark Kent?"

"Yes, Justin, the man of steel. Superman also wrote the three laws of robotics."

"Well if I had nano-dust floating around me, I'd tell it to turn into another beer."

"It doesn't work like that. You can tell it to be a cup but it can't just turn into beer."

"Fuck that then. Can I have another beer?"

"Yes, of course, grab another round for everyone. And check on Frank. He's been in there a while."

I rode with Frank in the ambulance on the way to the hospital. Yola and Justin followed in a taxi. Vomit had forced its way out of Frank's nose, down his esophagus, and into his lungs due to his mouth being blocked by the bandage. The paramedics placed a tube down his throat, pushing his bandaged tongue to the side. It pointed at me, smiling, for the entire trip. Even after they removed the tube.

"Is he alright?"
"No."
"What does that mean?"
"He died in the ambulance on the way here."
"Oh my god... wait, this isn't another joke, is it?"
"Why would I joke about something like... okay, yes, Frank's fine. They're keeping him overnight though."

.....................

From: Thomas de Masi
Date: Monday 3 September 2001 10.09am
To: David Thorne
Subject: Yola's email address

Hi David,

I hope this is the right email address. I was wondering if I could get Yola's number off you. I meant to get it Friday night but she left in a hurry. Thanks.

Tom de Masi

**From**: David Thorne
**Date**: Monday 3 September 2001 10.32am
**To**: Thomas de Masi
**Subject**: Re: Yola's email address

Hello Thomas,

It would be inappropriate for me to give out a staff member's contact details but I will certainly forward your email to Yola. That way she can contact you should she choose to do so. I've no doubt she will though; she hasn't stopped talking about you. I think she might have a bit of a crush.

Also, credit where credit's due; I saw the new STA bus livery design this morning and was quite impressed. It came out well. Congrats to you and your team.

Regards, David

........................................................................................

**From**: Thomas de Masi
**Date**: Monday 3 September 2001 11.12am
**To**: David Thorne
**Subject**: Re: Re: Yola's email address

Hi David,

Thank you very much. We worked hard on the liveries and are proud of the result. I will pass your kind words on to my team. I saw your work on the Yaldara labels a while back and was also impressed. We should have a beer sometime.

Tom de Masi

Thomas had a dozen long-stemmed roses delivered to our office address that afternoon. There was a card attached that read, '*Yola – Can't stop thinking about you. Tom*'. As Yola was out of the office when the courier arrived, I swapped the card out for one that read, '*Yola – Roses are red, violets are blue, I've got another news clipping I want to show you. Tom*'. I also had Frank whip up a quick 30% discount voucher for bus travel.

"Is this a joke? Did you send these?"

"No, I swear to you I didn't."

"He wants to show me another news clipping. What's that supposed to mean?"

"Maybe it's a euphemism."

"And there's a bus voucher attached."

"Someone's obviously smitten."

"It's weird..."

"You should probably email and thank him regardless."

"I don't know his email address."

"I'll send it to you, he emailed me earlier asking for your phone number."

'Are you serious? Did you give it to him?"

"No. Just your home address."

"What?"

"How else was he supposed to add you to the State Transport Authority's mailing list? You're all signed up to receive their monthly newsletter and a free subscription to *Ride!* Magazine."

**From**: David Thorne
**Date**: Tuesday 4 September 2001 10.10am
**To**: Neil Fairhead
**Subject**: Press Checks

Hello Neil,

Just letting you know we changed the yellow (PMS 121) to PMS 122 on press yesterday. With a spot varnish on the blue, PMS 121 was looking too light. It's a minor change and doesn't effect pricing or delivery. We will update the style guide accordingly.

I'll bring a few first run copies from yesterday's press check (and this afternoon's press check for the other artwork) with me to our meeting tomorrow. Delivery will be the day after but I thought you might like to see them earlier.

Regards, David

...............................................................................................................

**From**: Neil Fairhead
**Date**: Tuesday 4 September 2001 12.55pm
**To**: David Thorne
**Subject**: Re: Press Checks

Fantastic. Looking forward to our meeting tomorrow. Can't wait to see the final product.

We had a director meeting this morning and the printing invoice was approved. You should receive that within 14 days with the other one.

We also discussed the opportunity that I wanted to talk with you tomorrow about and I think you are going to be very pleased with the decision.

Neil Fairhead, Director
Southern Australia Shipping Company

. . . . . . . . . . . . . . . . . . .

I read somewhere that everyone's life can be broken into seven year segments - seven, fourteen, twenty-one, twenty-eight, etc. At each of these specific ages, an event - or a choice, or a mistake - changes the direction our lives take.

When I was seven, I waded out into the middle of our family pool holding a brick. Nobody else was home. I threw the brick into the air a few times, to test trajectory, then threw it high and stepped under it. My plan was that the brick would knock me out and I'd drown. Which would mean never having to go to school again.

The day before, during lunchtime at school, Peter Jackson pulled my shorts down in the cafeteria. My underpants went with them. I was holding a tray of food at the time and had coloured my penis with blue food colouring the night before. I've no idea why, it was probably just a boy thing. I've done a lot of stupid things with my penis since then and it was a long time ago so the specifics are hazy. I do remember that my hands were also stained blue, from the application, and I'd told kids that it was from eating blueberries.

It worked, in part; the brick knocked me out for a bit, but I was pulled out of the water by our elderly next-door neighbour, Mr Williams. He'd been raking leaves in his back yard, stopped to watch the whole production, then jumped the fence. Mrs Williams put Mercurochrome and a Band-aid on the small cut on my head while I sat on their kitchen counter wrapped in a towel. Mr Williams made me a cup of tea. He used two teabags, I remember as he used both hands to jiggle, and added lots of sugar and milk.

"Drink this."
"Thank you."
"What the fuck where you thinking? You could have died."
"It was an accident. I was just playing a game."
"Oh yes, the 'get in the pool and throw a brick in the air and step under it' game. I know it well. Were you practicing for the finals?"
"No. Just playing."
"Everything okay at home?"
"Yes."
"Why aren't you at school? Are you wagging it?"
"... no."
"Everything okay at school?"
"... yes."
"Some kids giving you a hard time?"
"Just Peter Jackson."
"Ah. Bit of playground bully is he?"
"No, it was in the cafeteria."
"What happened?"

"He pulled my pants down and everyone saw. Even Emma Jenkins."
"Walk it off, princess."

'Walk it off, princess' has kind of been my motto since. It might not seem like a very empathetic or kind response to someone's problems, but it actually is. It's the optimal response. It says 'It's a temporary issue and you'll be fine, don't worry about it. It'll take more than that to keep you down." Which might also work but it's a bit of a mouthful and hard to remember. Plus it doesn't have the princess bit.

My nickname at school for the next few years was Blueberry Dick but it could have been worse, there were kids in my class named Slop Bucket and Carrot Arse. Apparently Carrot Arse had put a baby carrot up his arse and it got stuck and he had to go to the hospital to have it removed but I have no idea how this rumour got started. Slop Bucket's nickname was originally Drip Tray - due to his severe facial acne that wept pus constantly - but became Slop Bucket after a lengthy discussion about the limited volume of fluid a drip tray could hold.

When I was fourteen, I let a middle aged record store owner take photos of my penis in the bathroom in exchange for a copy of Beastie Boys' *Licensed to Ill* on vinyl and two Depeche Mode tour t-shirts. It seemed like a good deal at the time and had no life changing ramifications so I should probably have thought of a better one for fourteen...

When I was fourteen, I had my heart broken for the first time. Her name was Emma Jenkins and I'd had a crush on her for years. Once, four or so years earlier, I'd pushed her on the playground swing. Just to start her off though; she did the legs-in-legs-out thing after that. She was wearing a blue Scrunchie that day and her hair smelled like bananas. We were paired to do a science class experiment together as Teresa, Emma's best friend and usual lab-partner, broke her neck and died at a public swimming pool the week before. The school held an assembly and talked to us about the dangers of diving into the shallow end and running on concrete so I was never sure which killed her. Maybe it was a combination of both.

I'd been stuck in a group of three with Hazardous Bog (formerly known as Slop Bucket) and Carrot Arse due to an odd number of students, so it worked out well for me. I had the entire scenario scripted within seconds; I'd be easy-going and funny and she'd laugh at my jokes. Later, one of her friends would tell me that she liked me and I'd let it be known that I liked her as well which would officially mean we were 'going out with each other'. We'd hold hands at recess and walk around the school with our hands in each other's back jeans pocket at lunch. I'd buy her one of those heart-shaped necklaces that you break in half and both wear and then she'd let me kiss her at the bus stop. I collected my notebook and *Knight Rider* pencil case and sat beside Emma, watched her push a blonde strand of hair behind her ear and raise a hand.

"Yes, Emma?"

"Why do I have to be lab partners with Blueberry?"

"Because there are only twelve Bunsen burners. It's a fifteen minute experiment, Emma, just put up with it."

'Well, Kate doesn't want to be partners with Brian, why can't Brian be his partner and Kate can be mine?"

"Fine."

It was my first time in detention. I thought it would be like a normal classroom with a teacher sitting up the front but it was just an empty conference room. Peter Jackson was also in detention that afternoon, for killing a duck in the creek behind the school. He had a bright red ear from being slapped by Mr Connerly, the gym teacher.

"Did you really kill a duck?"

"I had to. Its wing was all mangled."

"Maybe a vet could have put it in a cast."

"No, it was really fucked up. There were ants crawling all over it and it could hardly move."

"Did you at least kill it quickly?"

"Really quick. With a rock. I didn't want to but..."

"If I was dying and covered in ants, I'd want it to end quickly. My dad ran over my tortoise with the car a few years back and it was still alive so he cut its head off with a shovel."

"That's pretty sad. I like tortoises."

"Yeah, me too. Does your ear hurt?"

"Not really. What are you in here for?"

"Pouring a beaker of hydrogen peroxide on Emma Jenkins'

head."

"That's awesome."

"Is it?"

"Yes, she's a bitch. You should have used nitric acid. It's caustic."

"I kind of liked her. A lot. Since first grade."

"Walk it off, princess."

"Where did you hear that?"

"My dad used to say it. Do you like video games?"

"Yes."

"Have you ever smoked weed?"

"No."

"Do you want to come over my house after this to play video games and smoke weed?"

"Okay."

When I was twenty-one, I let myself in the back door of Peter Jackson's house and found him hanging by a rope in his kitchen. He'd used a length of yellow clothes line that had previously been strung between two trees in his backyard to dry laundry on. It was thin and had cut deep into his neck. His hands were also tied, then tied to his belt; two of the straps the belt passed through were ripped so he must have struggled hard when he kicked away the milk crate. His face looked similar to that scene in *Total Recall* when Arnold takes off his space helmet off on Mars - as if he was straining to push out a big poo. I thought it was a prank at first, I pushed him and he swayed back and forth for a while, slowly turning. There was a note in his back pocket. I lifted it out and read it, then screwed it up and put in my pocket. We usually hung out two or three times a week but he hadn't answered his phone since breaking up with his girlfriend of three years a few days before. I was with him when he learned Lisa was cheating, someone called him and said she was drunk at a party and was giving guys lap dances. We drove to a house full of bogans* in Klemzig** late at night and pulled up in the driveway. Guns N' Roses' *Paradise City* could be heard coming from the house and the people hanging out on the front porch looked pretty rough, but Peter stormed inside demanding to know where Lisa was. Someone pointed to a bedroom door and he threw it open to discover Lisa, on all fours, taking it from behind by an old guy wearing a hat. It was one of those hats like Crocodile Dundee wears. Lisa, facing away from the door and not even bothering to look around, yelled, "He's not finished yet."

"Walk it off, princess."
"Yeah."

When I was twenty-eight, I gave one-hundred and fifty-thousand dollars to a con artist.

---

* *As America has its trailer trash and England its chavs, so too does Australia. Easily identified by their high pitched greeting, "Oi, gimme sum fukken money for the bus brah or I'll fukken smash ya face in", these colourful characters serve as a community reminder of how low white people can sink.*

** *A low-income suburb of Adelaide, South Australia, where the odds of escaping with your wallet, a will to live, and without a needle-stick injury, are extremely slim.*

"It's a lot of money, Neil."

"It's an investment. One that guarantees a return of thirty-five percent in three months. That means your $150,000 will be worth $202,500 by November. You can either invest that for another three months and turn it into $273,375 or take it out. It's completely up to you."

"It's practically everything I have left in my savings account."

"How long did it take you to save that money?"

"Three years."

"Do you want to spend another three years designing brochures and stationery?"

"Can I have a few days to think it over?"

"Of course, if you need to. We all agreed in yesterday's director meeting to hold the spot open for you until the investor meeting on Friday. You just need to let us know before then."

"Don't get me wrong, I do appreciate the offer. It's just a lot of money. Especially at the moment. We lost our main client recently and... well, I won't go into that but..."

"There was also talk about bringing you on as a director. We need someone to oversee the branding and marketing of *Southern Australis* and while it's just a paper title, it comes with a budget that would keep your agency in work for years. We received backing from the Australian Tourism Board yesterday, which means billboards, television advertising, tourism magazine adverts..."

"Nobody would have to fend for themselves in a forest."

"Sorry?"

"I'll have a cashier's cheque for you this afternoon."

I've made thousands of mistakes in my life. Everyone has. It's part of what makes us who we are. Sometimes the mistakes make us better people, sometimes they leave scars. There's mistakes between the two ends of the 'mistake scale' of course - the silly mistakes, like washing a wayward red sock with white sheets or leaving a car window down during a rainstorm - but these are hardly worth mentioning. Certainly not every time you offer to do the laundry or take someone's car to the shops because they parked behind you.

One of the lies we tell ourselves about our mistakes is, "my biggest mistake was trusting $x$." This implies fault lies with $x$ and, as trust is generally seen as a positive character trait, is really just presenting ourselves with a little medal. A purple heart for betrayal. There are probably a million different reasons why we trust people but most of them are selfish reasons; we require something from them - companionship, validation, hope, or security...

I trusted Neil Fairhead because a week before I met with him, I sat at my desk at 2am drafting an email to Frank, Yola, Justin and Huang, apologising for failing them, for cowardly sending them an email instead of looking them in the face, for it ending up this way... And because I didn't want to design stationery and brochures for the next three years - if we even lasted that long. After the SASC work wound down, I'd need to seek out more clients, more brochure and stationery commissions, and the email would be sitting in my drafts folder, waiting.

**From**: David Thorne
**Date**: Tuesday 10 September 2001 9.34am
**To**: Neil Fairhead
**Subject**: Investment contract

Hello Neil,

I hope Friday's meeting last week went well.

I was reading the investment contract and it lists Onkourse Pty Ltd as the company name - not Southern Australia Shipping Company - from page 3 onwards. Is this an error?

Regards, David

......................................................................................................

**From**: Neil Fairhead
**Date**: Tuesday 10 September 2001 12.55pm
**To**: David Thorne
**Subject**: Re: Investment contract

David,

Thanks for letting me know. Yes that should be SASC. I will get an amended contract to you this week.

Neil Fairhead, Director
Southern Australia Shipping Company

**From**: David Thorne
**Date**: Monday 24 September 2001 9.34am
**To**: Neil Fairhead
**Subject**: Re: Re: Investment contract

Hello Neil,

We've been working on the website design for the last week and should have something to show you by Friday. I've received samples of crew uniforms and big puffy jackets. The embroidered patches look great.

Do you have an ETA for when the ship arrives in port next week? At this point we are planning to meet with Don Prime from Option[a] on-site to go over signage requirements and Mary Harben's people can meet us a day or two after to measure for the livery. I need to lock in dates for both.

My staff also asked if it would be possible to be at the docks when the ship pulls into port. We're all excited to see it.

Also, I haven't received the amended investor contract. Have you had a chance to look at that? We are also yet to receive payment for either the deposit or printing. It's been 20 days since I was told it had been sent to accounts so if you could also check on that I'd appreciate it.

To be perfectly honest, without those payments being received and cleared by Thursday, I will have difficulty making payroll for my staff this month.

Regards, David

**From**: David Thorne
**Date**: Thursday 27 September 2001 2.16pm
**To**: Neil Fairhead
**Subject**: Invoices

Neil,

Can you give me a call? I left a message yesterday but haven't heard back from you. Thanks.

David

......................

**From**: David Thorne
**Date**: Tuesday 2 October 2001 7.58am
**To**: Neil Fairhead
**Subject**: Contact

Neil,

Can you call me today please? I've left a couple of messages on your office answering machine. Your phone rings out. Still chasing those invoices and I have Don Prime and Mary Harben waiting to lock in dates. What day does the ship arrive?

I realise this is a busy time for you but I had to make payroll using my credit card on Friday and need those invoices cleared this week.

David

There's a 'current affairs' television show that airs weekdays in Australia called *Today Tonight*. I haven't seen it in a few years but I assume it's the same format; people contact the producers of *Today Tonight* and have a bitch about a company not giving them a refund for faulty goods or something, and Frank Pangallo, an investigative journalist, rushes to the business with a bunch of television cameras to get to the bottom of the problem. Often, the perplexed business owner will be like, "What the fuck? Yes, we sold him the kayak but how is it our fault if he didn't strap it to the top of his car properly? No, we're not giving a refund for a flat kayak with truck tire marks all over it but it was nice meeting you, Frank. I watch you on the telly all the time."

I saw one episode where they hid in a van and filmed for three days to catch an elderly woman who was letting her dog shit on another neighbours lawn and not picking it up. When she saw Frank and the cameramen pile out of the van, she legged it but fell and broke her hip. Occasionally, however, they turn up at a legitimately dodgy business and the owner runs from the cameras and puts his hand over the lens when they catch up. Sometimes they push the camera away and Frank yells, "Don't touch the camera, that's assault!" and the owner yells, "I asked you to leave!" and Frank replies, "What do you have to say to the family you ripped off? Will they get their money back for the driveway paving they paid for but never received?"

It's all pretty stupid but the program reaches a decent-sized audience. I used to watch it fairly regularly. I was watching it the night Neil Fairhead was on.

"Hello, Neil? Frank Pangallo from *Today Tonight*."

"Yes, I know who you are. I'm not interested in talking to..."

"We just want to talk to you about the Southern Australian Shipping Company, Neil."

"I'm busy at the moment. I'll have to ask you to leave..."

"What do you have to say to the hundreds of investors that believed they were investing in a ship?"

"There is a ship. Look, I've asked you to leave. This is my home, you're welcome to set up an appointment at my office if you want to discuss this like civi..."

"You don't have an office, Neil. We checked and that property is still the registered address of Onkourse, which is currently under investigation by the Australian Securities and Investments Commission, but your lease expired last year. It's now a bakery. Where's the ship, Neil?"

"We're currently under discussion with the owners of a decommissioned Russian ice-breaker about purchasing..."

"There is no ship, is there Neil?"

"Yes, there is."

"Your glossy brochure, which is very nice I must say, states that you have the backing of the Australian Geographic Society. They've never heard of you, Neil."

"I've asked you to leave. I'm going to call the police if you don't leave my property immediately."

"This isn't even a real ship in the brochure. The name and logo have been Photoshopped onto it and this picture of people on the ice wearing red jackets with the ship's logo added to the sleeve is from a 1987 mining expedition in Norway."

"We commissioned an agency to do th..."

"You keep saying 'we', Neil. Who's we?"

"SASC."

"That's just you. You're under investigation by ASIC for six separate businesses; Earn and Learn, Brink, Netlink, eBoxes, the National Internet Services Provider Network, and Onkourse - and you were the sole proprietor of every one. You're a con man, Neil."

"No, I'm not."

"What would you call yourself then, Neil? A thief? You defrauded Aussie-battlers of almost a million dollars."

"No, I didn't. I'm still in discussion with ASIC about those other businesses, I wasn't even a director of th..."

"Are you moving, Neil?"

"...I've asked you to leave several times and I'm going to lose my patience in a..."

"They look like moving boxes. Where are you moving to, Neil?"

"None of your fucking business."

The word 'fucking' was beeped out because the show aired at 6.30pm. There were a few more beeps as Neil pushed the camera away and slammed the door closed. Frank yelled through the door for Neil to come out and finish the conversation but Neil ignored him.

My phone rang during the program - shortly after the part where Neil answered the door looking startled - but I ignored it. It rang several times more before I answered.

"Did you watch *Today Tonight*?"

"Yes, Frank."

"Neil Fairhead was on it."

"I know."

"What does this mean?"

"I don't know."

"There's no ship?"

"I don't know."

"I don't reckon there is a ship. He said he's been talking with someone about purchasing one, not that it's already paid for and is on its way here. His office is a bakery. I think it was all a con. Is he going to pay us for all the work we did?"

"I don't know."

"What about the printing?"

"I don't know, Frank."

"This is bullshit. What are we going to do?"

"I don't know."

"I'm going to call Yola. I'll see you tomorrow."

"No, don't come in tomorrow, Frank. I'll email you. I'll email everyone."


I wasn't the worst hit of course, others had invested more money. Some had invested their life's savings. A couple invested just 45K but they were in their seventies and mortgaged their house to raise the money. It's easy to convince people of anything when you have the right marketing materials. There was no ship, no directors, no backing from the Australian Geographic Society or Tourism Board. Just a shit-ton of lies and glossy brochures.

Neil moved to Queensland, the sunshine state, and set up other businesses. I read a news article years later about one of them, an online advertising business called EasyFind, that folded owing tens of thousands to staff and several hundreds of thousands to the Australian Taxation Office. I spent several thousand in lawyers fees, and months in courtrooms, but all I received for my efforts was 2.8 cents on the dollar and, for the record, the following communication:

**From**: Ronald Davies
**Date**: Monday 8 April 2002 11.19am
**To**: David Thorne
**Subject**: Case 017029031 /Neil Fairhead

Dear Mr. Thorne.

The Australian Securities and Investments Commission (ASIC) has accepted two enforceable undertakings from Mr. Neil Harvey John Fairhead.

Mr. Fairhead has undertaken not to be a company officer or to participate in the management of a corporation for ten years. He has also undertaken that he will not, in the future, directly or indirectly give investment advice or be involved in a securities business or sell or promote investment in any scheme or project.

I have attached a copy of the enforceable undertaking for your records.

Ronald Davies, Investigations Officer, ASIC

AUSTRALIAN SECURITIES
& INVESTMENTS COMMISSION

017029031

## A S I C

Australian Securities & Investments Commission

### ENFORCEABLE UNDERTAKING

### AUSTRALIAN SECURITIES & INVESTMENTS COMMISSION

**Section 93AA Australian Securities & Investments Commission Act 2001**

**The commitments in this Undertaking are offered to the Australian Securities and Investments Commission ("ASIC") by:**

### Neil Harvey John Fairhead

Formerly of;              now of;
1 Seaview Avenue          1 Rutherglen Court
Hallett Cove SA 5158      Aroona Qld 4551

### Background

1  Neil Harvey John Fairhead ("Neil Fairhead") was from 31 March 1998 to 23 August 2000, a director of Onkourse Pty Ltd ACN 061 000 646 ("Onkourse") which traded as Oncourse Resource Group and Oncourse Financial Group. From 14 January 2000 to 14 December 2000 Neil Fairhead was a director of Brink Technology Pty Ltd ACN 091 194 937 ("Brink"). He has been from 20 October 1999 and is currently a director of Earn & Learn (Educational Systems) Pty Ltd ACN 090 045 088 ("Earn & Learn").

2  From 21 July 1993 until it was placed under external administration in February 2001, Onkourse operated a financial services business. From about 31 March 1998, Onkourse's business included mortgage refinancing and arranging a line of credit, arranging insurance, accounting services, business development and wealth creation .Under the banner of its wealth creation activities, Onkourse sought investment funds from its clients - and others - for specific purposes or schemes.

3  ASIC is investigating the activities of Onkourse and persons and entities associated with Onkourse and ASIC is of the view that this fundraising was carried out in contravention of Chapter 5C of the Corporations Law.

4  Some of the fundraising was for schemes external to Onkourse and its associates, including schemes known as Netlink, Eboxes, The Southern Australia Shipping Company Pty Ltd ACN 086 259 145 ("SASCO") and National Internet Service

Provider Project ("NISPP"); other fundraising was conducted for schemes or entities associated with Onkourse or its directors, including Earn and Learn and Brink.

5   Monies received by Onkourse, including fees and commissions and investor funds were frequently paid into Onkourse's operating account and applied without regard to the origin of the funds and the purpose for which they were received. Although ultimately several of the schemes received approximately the amount of funds raised for that purpose, Onkourse's books and records did not distinguish or separate the funds or reflect to whose account the funds should be credited.

6   Money was paid from Onkourse's account on a needs basis, whether for Onkourse's activities, director's fees and expenses or investment funds including investment funds for Earn & Learn and Brink. Onkourse's books do not clearly set out how much was raised and how much was paid out to each scheme entity, although it is clear that not all investor monies raised for these schemes went into the schemes.

7   In particular in relation to NISPP, a total of $377,500 appears to have been raised, the scheme did not proceed, and the investment funds were dissipated in Onkourse's operational costs.

8   In addition, when NISPP investors sought refunds, some were offered a profit share in Brink in lieu of a refund. Brink received no money in exchange for that right. Neil Fairhead was a director of both Brink and Onkourse at the time of this arrangement.

9   In particular, ASIC is concerned that:

9.1   Meetings of Onkourse, Earn & Learn and Brink usually took place together and although it is claimed that the meetings took place sequentially, it is clear from the minutes that the business of the three companies was dealt with in a conglomerate manner

9.2   Funds of Onkourse, Earn & Learn and Brink, together with investors funds for other projects were intermingled in Onkourse's operating account;.

9.3   From at least July 2000 Onkourse was not generating enough in fees and Commissions to meet its outgoings and was using investor funds as operating capital;

9.4   From at least July 2000 Onkourse was trading whilst insolvent;

9.5   The affairs of Onkourse, Earn and Learn and Brink were not carried out with the required level of care and diligence by the directors,

9.6   Brink has suffered detriment from its officers offering interests in Brink without any consideration moving to Brink in return therefore;

181

9.7  The financial records of Onkourse, Earn and Learn and Brink do not adequately
set out those companies' financial position

10  Neil Fairhead acknowledges ASIC's concerns set out above.

## Undertakings

11  Pursuant to Section 93AA of the Australian Securities and Investments
Commission Act 2001, Neil Fairhead hereby undertakes:

11.1  For a period of ten years from the date of hereof, alternatively, from the date after
the expiration of 5 years from the date hereof that Neil Fairhead satisfies the
Assistant Director of Enforcement for ASIC's Adelaide office that he has
successfully completed the Institute of Company Director's course for company
directors, or an equivalent course approved by ASIC:

  11.1.1  not to be involved in the management of a corporation, other than Earn &
  Learn (Educational Systems ) Pty Ltd ;

  11.1.2  not to do any act as an officer of a corporation other than  Earn & Learn
  (Educational Systems ) Pty Ltd ;

  11.1.3  not to apply or permit another to apply on his behalf to be registered as a
  director of a corporation.

11.2  During the period of this undertaking, to advise the Assistant Director,
Enforcement, of ASIC's Adelaide office of any change in business of Earn & Learn
(Educational Systems) Pty Ltd from the promotion and sale of its "Pocket Pal" product.

## Acknowledgements

12  Neil Fairhead acknowledges that:

  12.1  ASIC may issue a media release on execution of this undertaking referring
  to its terms and the concerns of ASIC which lead to its execution;

  12.2  ASIC may from time to time publicly refer to this undertaking

12.3  ASIC will make this undertaking available for public inspection

13     Neil Fairhead acknowledges that ASIC's acceptance of this undertaking in no
       way derogates from the rights and remedies available to ASIC or any other
       person arising from any conduct described in this undertaking.

14     Neil Fairhead acknowledges that ASIC's acceptance of an enforceable
       undertaking does not affect ASIC's power to investigate a contravention arising
       from future conduct, or pursue criminal prosecution, or its power to lay charges
       or seek a pecuniary civil order.

15     Neil Fairhead acknowledges that this undertaking has no operative force until
       accepted by ASIC.

SIGNED by: ....................................
**Neil Harvey John Fairhead**

This      day of      03 ·      2002

In the presence of:

..........................................
Witness:

......CARY S PUDDY..........
Name: (print)

......8ᵗ Floor, 100 PIRIE S ADELAIDE 5000
Address:

ACCEPTED BY the Australian       )
Securities & Investments         )
Commission pursuant to the       )
ASIC Act 2001 section 93AA by its )
duly authorised delegate         )

..........................................
Karen Axford
Regional Commissioner South Australia
Australian Securities & Investments Commission

This 12ᵗʰ day of   March ,    2002

183

**From**: David Thorne
**Date**: Monday 8 April 2002 1.04pm
**To**: Ronald Davies
**Subject**: Re: Case 017029031 /Neil Fairhead

Dear Ronald,

Thank you for your email.

I've read through the attached document and, from what I can tell, ASIC's enforceable undertaking boils down to, "That was a bit naughty, don't do it again."

Please correct me if I'm wrong.

Regards, David

........................................................................................

**From**: Ronald Davies
**Date**: Monday 8 April 2002 1.41pm
**To**: David Thorne
**Subject**: Re: Re: Case 017029031 /Neil Fairhead

Dear Mr. Thorne,

The enforceable undertaking means Mr. Fairhead can no longer operate a financial or investment business or offer financial or investment services. Yes, it boils down to (an enforceable) don't do it again but there are penalties if he fails to comply.

Ronald Davies, Investigations Officer, ASIC

**From**: David Thorne
**Date**: Monday 8 April 2002 2.01pm
**To**: Ronald Davies
**Subject**: Re: Re: Re: Case 017029031 /Neil Fairhead

Dear Ronald,

Thank you clarifying.

I have a basement full of abducted children that I was planning to sell into slavery but I was concerned about the repercussions of such.

Knowing that the only punishment, if caught, will be that I will no longer be allowed to abduct children and sell them into slavery is a huge relief.

I'm offering a two for one special on under-fives at the moment if you're interested.

Regards, David

....................................................................................................

**From**: Ronald Davies
**Date**: Monday 8 April 2002 2.16pm
**To**: David Thorne
**Subject**: Re: Re: Re: Re: Case 017029031 /Neil Fairhead

David,

For what it's worth, people like Mr. Fairhead eventually get what is coming to them. Until then, it is what it is.

Ronald

"It is what it is" is basically another version of "Walk it off, princess" but you'll sound like an Amish farmer if you use it in conversation.

"And then she told everyone in the meeting that she thinks the new location should have a rock-tile wall behind the counter from local quarries. Which was my idea. She just stole it and pretended she'd had some kind of interior decorating vision. Who does she think she is?"
"It is what it is."
"What's that supposed to mean?"
"Winds a'pickin up."
"What?"
"Storms a'comin. We'll hoffe to have the barn beams redd before tonight's affirmation of the Ordnung."

Yes, I Googled 'things Amish people say' to write the sentence above. I found a whole list of Amish words and can now curse in Pennsylvanian Dutch; "Boss a'dog hex" translates to, "Kiss a dead witch."

I've never met an actual Amish person but there's lots of Mennonites in the region of Virginia I currently live in. Mennonites have similar religious beliefs to the Amish, they're both Anabaptist sects, but when it came to the whole 'not owning cars, laptops or mobile phones' thing, the Mennonites decided, "We're allowed to have them as long as we only use them while we're wearing a special outfit. Just the women have to wear the outfit though."

On my first trip to Virginia from Australia, Holly took to me a bunch of caves called The Luray Caverns. Caves are alright, I don't have posters on my wall about them or anything but I'm fine visiting one every twenty years or so. To ensure the natural beauty lasts for generations to come, most caverns protect and preserve their rock formations but Luray Caverns decided they'd lop off dozens of their stalactites at varying heights and install little hammers that remotely activate in sequence to play a tune. It's called The Great Stalac'pipe' Organ. I wish I was making this up. After standing around awkwardly listening to *Popcorn* in an echoey chamber with our tour group - some of which were wearing ankle length floral dresses and a weird bun-hat which I just put down to local fashion* - Holly leant in and whispered, "Look, Mennonites."

Having subscribed to a rock collecting magazine that came with a different mineral each month (and a free binder) when I was ten, I loudly declared, "That's Calcite, not Mennonite. What the fuck is Mennonite?"

---

* *Virginia's fashion might be described as eclectic, vibrant and happening but only by people who use those kind of words and live somewhere else and thought the person asking was referring to Virginia who works in accounting. The official costume of the state of Virginia is Mossy Oak® Realtree® hunting apparel with Scent Block® technology and a 40-ounce bottle of Steel Reserve Malt Liquor. For men, the same but with a beard. New Market in Virginia has it's own official costume consisting of sweat-pants pulled up around the chest, a red cap featuring meaningless political statements, and a barrel of cheese-balls.*

Yola received a job offer from Mary Harben Design a week after we shut everything down and we kept in contact for a few years until she married a guy she met on the Internet and moved to Albania. She sent me a camera-phone picture of herself holding an AK47 and a hookah outside a mud hut and I sent her one back of Frank and I holding up glasses of beer at the *Grace Emily* and giving her the finger. Her husband replied asking me not to contact her again because it was inappropriate for her to have male friends. She's probably a member of ISIS or something now.

Frank applied for a deckhand position on a cabin cruiser he'd read about while doing research for the SASC project and, years later, made bosun. He sent me a picture of himself standing on a deck in a white uniform with turquoise waters behind him and text that read, "My office." I sent him one back of my office at de Masi jones - it showed a messy desk covered in brochure and stationery proofs - and one of Seb eating corn in the bath.

I didn't keep in contact with Huang, as she stole my Playstation and dance mat when she left, but Justin and I caught up fairly regularly. He taught himself to code and we collaborated on the interface and graphics for a couple of shareware games. We went halves in the profits and made around twenty dollars a week until a Japanese software company purchased the rights to *Battle-Beetle* for eighty-thousand dollars and later released it under the name *Mushiking: The King of Beetles* on the Nintendo DS.

I paid off my credit cards, Justin moved to Sydney* (for love) and made a name for himself writing analytical software that tracked statistics in real time. In 2008, he sold a predictive modeling program he'd written to a company called Omniture for $4.5 million (and $2.5 million in assumed vested stock options) and Adobe Systems purchased Omniture a year later for $1.8 billion. I like to imagine Justin purchased a shit-ton of Christmas lights with the money.

I looked up Neil Fairhead on Facebook while I was writing this article; his profile picture shows him and his Fijian wife smiling happily. His red hair is grey now and he has a matching little goatee. I have a few grey hairs myself. I pluck them out but they keep coming back. Holly told me that if I pluck out a grey hair, two will grow, but she also once bought one of those wax ear trumpet candles that you stick in your ear and light to ward off evil spirits or something so her scientific knowledge is questionable at best.

I considered, for a moment, messaging Neil to ask if he felt bad for the elderly couple who lost their home, for the people who lost their life's savings, for taking everything I had - or if he simply saw himself as deserving of our money because he was smarter than us, because we were gullible fools for

* *I can't remember why Justin moved to Sydney but I thought you might read that sentence and wonder why so I added this asterisk thing. Justin did send me a photo of himself standing in front of the Sydney Harbour Bridge with a fat gothic girl so perhaps it was for love. I'm just going to say it was for love.*

believing him. It's possible of course that given enough investors, Neil fully intended to buy a ship. That the lies were a means to an end and if enough people believed that he owned a ship, and enough of those people invested in that belief, he would own a ship. Perhaps to him, the difference between 'do' and 'will' was semantics. Or perhaps it was all bullshit. The money wasn't held in a 'special ship savings account', it went to the mortgage on his Queensland property and his E-Class Mercedes and his Malibu speedboat - all in his wife's name. Most of Neil's Facebook posts are blocked from public view but his wife's profile is full of photos of the two of them holidaying in Fiji and other exotic locations. There's one of Neil sitting on a jet-ski holding his thumb and little finger out in the 'gnarly' gesture. He's wearing a tank top that says Island Life and his cap is on backwards like the cool kids wear them. He probably has to order them made to his size. One of the photos shows his wife leaning against a Porsche with the text, "Vinaka Siganisucu e sega ni mudu, kemuni tagane vakawati dau lomana!" which roughly translates to, "Best birthday gift ever, love you husband!"

I can curse in Fijian now; "Biuta na baleka nomu boto, dautane" means, "Shove a coconut up your arse, whore."
She blocked me; which is understandable as it was pretty immature.

Holly frowned and held up an A4 page from a freshly printed stack, "Is that it?"

"Is what it?"

"This story about Neil Fairhead. You just ended it on the bit about his wife shoving a coconut up her butt. She didn't even have anything to do with the story."

"No, I ended it saying everything turned out fine in the end."

"Not really, he got away with it."

"Yes, he got away with it, but there wasn't much we could do about it so we all walked it off. It's like an Aesop's tale."

"No, it isn't."

"Yes, it is. It's like that one about the fox and the crow. The one where they have a race. It's about moving on."

"The fox and the crow don't have a race. The crow has cheese and the fox wants it so the fox convinces the crow that he wants to hear her beautiful singing voice and the crow opens her beak to sing and drops the cheese."

"Exactly, it's about letting things go."

"No, it isn't. It's about flattery."

"What's the one about grapes then?"

"What?"

"The one about having to get a fox and a sheep and some grapes across a river but only two can fit in the boat at the same time."

"That's not an Aesop's tale. Besides, telling Neil's wife to shove a coconut up her butt is hardly moving on or letting go. It just comes across as if you're still cross and haven't walked anything off at all."

"That's a valid point. I'll have to remember to delete that bit as it does kind of undermine the serendipitous message."

"There's a serendipitous message? Where?"

"Everywhere. If it hadn't have been for Neil, I wouldn't have taken the design director position at de Masi jones, which means I wouldn't have started a stupid website, which means I wouldn't have met you. Frank probably wouldn't have become a bosun and Justin might not have designed software that made him a multi-millionaire."

"Yola married a mean Albanian man."

"Not right away, after working for me, she went to work for Mary Harben which was quite a step up. She didn't marry the Albanian man until years later. Also, I think he might have actually been Armenian. Or maybe Turkish. He definitely had a moustache."

"You said she's probably a member of ISIS now and you didn't even mention what happened to Huang."

"I was joking about the ISIS thing and I saw Huang a few years later at a trade show for new food products. I designed the packaging for a client's range of crackers that were being exhibited and went to take photos of their booth and saw her there."

"Doing what?"

"Flogging jars of homemade Chinese simmer sauce. She gave me one and I told her the label was shit and she told me I was stupid. Her product ended up getting shelf space in supermarkets so I assume she made out okay."

"You should have included that, it's nice to know."

"Bitch stole my Playstation."

"Well at least add a bit at the end about how if you hadn't met Neil you wouldn't have met me. That would be a much happier ending."

"Not everything has to be about you, Holly."

"It never is."

"Walk it off, princess."

# About the Author

David Thorne is a precocious but outgoing child known for his avant-garde day-glo and multicolored attire, along with his pigtails. His father walked out on his family, then his mother abandoned him at a Chicago shopping center, leaving David alone with his dog Brandon. Afterwards, David discovered a vacant apartment in a local building.

The building was managed by Henry Warnimont - an elderly, widowed photographer with a grouchy streak. David hit it off with young Cherie Johnson, who lived in Henry's building with her grandmother Betty. Henry discovered David in the empty apartment across from his, and listened to his story. The relationship between the two blossomed, despite red tape from social workers, and Henry applied to the courts to become David's foster father. As their day in court approached, the state forced David to stay at Fenster Hall, a shelter for orphaned and abandoned children, which made him realize how close he had grown to Henry. Finally, their day in court arrived, and the court approved Henry to become David's foster father. Shortly after, Henry's downtown photography studio was destroyed in a fire and it seemed for a time that he would not be able to recover from its aftermath and resume his career. As a result of his stress, Henry ended up hospitalized from a bleeding ulcer.

During this time, Betty and Cherie made arrangements for David to stay with them until Henry recovered. Everyone's stability was halted when bureaucratic social worker Simon Chillings showed up, found out about Henry's condition, and deemed the worst: he found Betty unsuitable to care for David, because she was a single woman with long working hours, already raising her granddaughter. Chillings also felt that Henry was unfit to be David's legal guardian in the long term - due to his health, age, and uncertain financial future. Chillings made David a ward of the state yet again, and he returned to Fenster Hall. David's many efforts to escape from Fenster included a trick pulled by a friend, in which they dressed up and pretended to be David. Chillings placed David with a new foster family: the fabulously wealthy Jules and Tiffany Buckworth, the latter of whom did not take kindly at all to David's working-class playfulness. Things gradually returned to normal: Henry, back on his feet following surgery, opened up a glitzy new studio at the local mall; in the process, he reunited with David and officially adopted him.

As David embarked on junior high, his avant-garde day-glo and multicolored attire segued into more traditional teenage styles, and his declaration of, and reliance on "David Power!" gave way to the realization that intelligence, common sense and a strong will can get one out of any problem. David's spunk and vivacious attitude toward life did remain though, thanks in part to the most important man in his life, his adoptive dad.

Henry's photography studio at the mall continued to see much success, so much that he received an offer from the magnate of Glossy's, a photo studio franchise, for a $100,000 buyout, which also included the offer of Henry becoming manager of the Glossy's location. Henry accepted, but soon found that his creativity was not being appreciated by his new employers. He quit Glossy's and invested his money in a hamburger restaurant which he called David's Place.

David's dog Brandon fell in love with Brenda, a golden retriever who belonged to one of Henry and David's neighbours. Their whirlwind romance culminated in a wedding ceremony in the courtyard, which was mostly attended by other neighbourhood canines.

Books by the Same Author

# The Internet is a Playground

ISBN 978-1585428816

Featuring over 200 pages of emails and articles from 27bslash6, plus over 160 pages of new material, and debuting at #4 on *The New York Times* Best Seller list, *The Internet is a Playground* is the first release by David Thorne. It makes a nice present, protects against tigers, and can be read while hiding in small places.

"There is usually a fine line between genius and insanity, but in this case it has become very blurred. Some of the funniest and most clever writing I have read in years."

*WIRED Magazine*

Books by the Same Author

# I'll Go Home Then;
# It's Warm and Has Chairs

ISBN 978-0-9886895-3-4

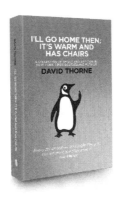

More emails, more articles, more exclusive content. *I'll Go Home Then; It's Warm and Has Chairs* is the second bestselling release by author David Thorne.

"Simultaneously stupid and brilliant. An astonishingly funny second book by the author of *The Internet is a Playground*."

*The Huffington Post*

Books by the Same Author

# Look Evelyn,
# Duck Dynasty Wiper Blades.
# We should Get Them

**ISBN** 978-0-9886895-2-7

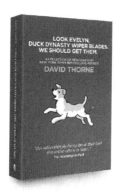

Featuring all new, never before published material, *Look Evelyn, Duck Dynasty Wiper Blades. We Should Get Them* is the bestselling third release by author David Thorne.

"Instantly engaging and very funny. Those new to Thorne's unique brand of humour are in for a real treat."

*Good Reads*

Books by the Same Author

# That's Not How You Wash a Squirrel

ISBN 978-0-9886895-9-6

*That's Not How You Wash a Squirrel* is the fourth release by *New York Times* bestselling author David Thorne and features over two hundred pages of brand new, never before seen essays and emails including: Ride of the Valkyries, Squirrel, Deer Camp, Tomotes, Gypsies, Cloud Backgrounds and many more.

"Clever and funny. Packed with stories and correspondences that will leave you chuckling long after you have finished them."

*The Washington Post*

## Books by the Same Author

# Wrap It In a Bit of Cheese Like You're Tricking the Dog

ISBN 978-0-9886895-5-8

The fifth release by *New York Times* bestselling author David Thorne featuring over two hundred pages of brand new, never before seen essays and emails including: Production Meeting, Robert the Telemarketing Raccoon, Mrs Gillespie, Smiling & Nodding, Ughhh, Raymond, and many more. Foreword by Patti Ford *Insane In The Mom Brain*

"Clever, awkward and laugh-out-loud funny."

*The Huffington Post*

Also Available

# The Ducks in the Bathroom Are Not Mine

ISBN 978-0-9886895-6-5

Limited Anniversary Edition.
Ten years of 27b/6 (2007 to 2017) in one huge 370 page
collectors volume celebrating
ten years of 27B/6

"A massive volume featuring a decades worth of
Thorne's best viral emails."

*Publisher's Weekly*

Also Available

# The Collected Works *of* 27b/6
# Victorian Edition

ISBN 978-0-9886895-1-0

All the 27b/6 articles in one volume - illustrated and abridged for polite society. Sure to be a hit at your next local council meeting or church fundraiser, *The Collected Works of 27b/6 ~ Victorian Edition* will take pride of place on your bookshelf next to the dictionary you don't remember buying and the rock that might be a meteorite. Free sticker with signed copies.

"So it's stories from your books and website edited down to a paragraph each? That's kind of stupid."

*Holly Thorne*

Also Available

# David Thorne Hums the Theme from Space 1999

## And Other Christmas Classics

ASIN B01FRFSTOQ / 60 minute CD

Forged almost entirely from thermoplastic polymers, this CD contains over 26 popular Christmas tracks including the theme from that movie about the big boat and that other one about the two guys.

"You need to get a life. I listened to about 1 second of it and threw it in the bin. Don't send me your stupid shit and I expect the stuff about me on the website to be deleted. I spoke to a lawyer and he said I could sue you for defamation."

*Lucius Thaller*